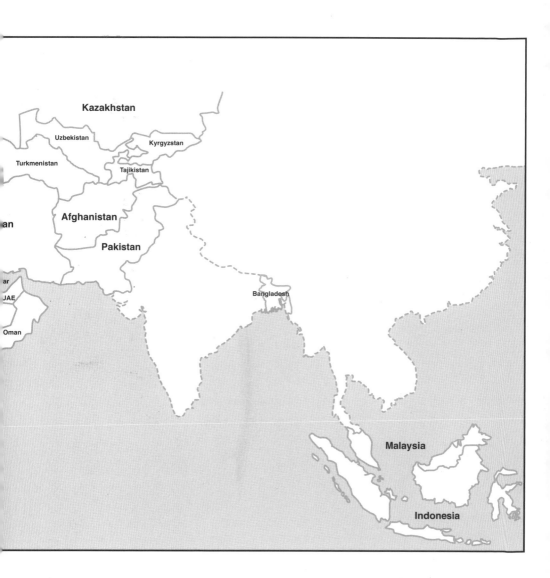

Praise for
Bernard Lewis

"Bernard Lewis, the master of the Middle East universe!"
—Les Gelb, former president, Council on Foreign Relations

"It is clear the author is one of two things: either a candid friend or an honorable enemy. And, in either case, he is one who disdains to dist the truth."
—Preface to the Arabic translation of Lewis' *The Middle East and the West*, published by the Muslim Brothers

"For newcomers to the subject…Bernard Lewis is the man."
—*TIME Magazine*

"The doyen of Middle Eastern studies."
—*The New York Times*

"No one writes about Muslim history with greater authority, or intel or literary charm."
—British historian Hugh Trevor-Roper

"Bernard Lewis has no living rival in his field."
—*Al Ahram*, Cairo (the most influential Arab world newspaper)

"When it comes to Islamic studies, Bernard Lewis is the father of us With brilliance, integrity, and extraordinary mastery of languages sources, he has led the way for…investigators seeking to understar Muslim world."
—*National Review*

"Bernard Lewis combines profound depth of scholarship with ency knowledge of the Middle East and, above all, readability."
—*Daily Telegraph* (London)

"Lewis speaks with authority in prose marked by lucidity, elegance wit and force."
—*Newsday* (New York)

"Lewis' style is lucid, his approach, objective."
—*Philadelphia Inquirer*

"Lewis writes with unsurpassed erudition and grace."
—*Washington Times*

ISLAM

ISLAM

THE RELIGION AND THE PEOPLE

BERNARD LEWIS

BUNTZIE ELLIS CHURCHILL

Ⅲ Wharton School Publishing

© 2009 by Pearson Education, Inc.
Publishing as Wharton School Publishing
Upper Saddle River, New Jersey 07458

Wharton School Publishing offers excellent discounts on this book when ordered in quantity for bulk purchases or special sales. For more information, please contact U.S. Corporate and Government Sales, 1-800-382-3419, corpsales@pearsontech-group.com. For sales outside the U.S., please contact International Sales at international@pearson.com.

Printed in the United States of America

Third Printing February 2009

ISBN-10 0-13-223085-2
ISBN-13 978-0-13-223085-8

Pearson Education LTD.
Pearson Education Australia PTY, Limited.
Pearson Education Singapore, Pte. Ltd.
Pearson Education North Asia, Ltd.
Pearson Education Canada, Ltd.
Pearson Educatión de Mexico, S.A. de C.V.
Pearson Education—Japan
Pearson Education Malaysia, Pte. Ltd.

Library of Congress Cataloging-in Publication Data

Lewis, Bernard, 1916-
  Islam : the religion and the people / Bernard Lewis, Buntzie Churchill.
    p. cm.
  ISBN 0-13-223085-2 (hardcover : alk. paper) 1. Islam--21st century. 2. Islam--Essence, genius, nature. 3. Religious awakening--Islam. I. Churchill, Buntzie, 1939- II. Title.
  BP161.3.L482 2008
  297--dc22
                    2008023257

Vice President, Publisher
Tim Moore

Associate Publisher and Director of Marketing
Amy Neidlinger

Wharton Editor
Yoram (Jerry) Wind

Operations Manager
Gina Kanouse

Digital Marketing Manager
Julie Phifer

Publicity Manager
Laura Czaja

Assistant Marketing Manager
Megan Colvin

Front Cover Design
MVB Design

Managing Editor
Kristy Hart

Senior Project Editor
Lori Lyons

Copy Editor
Anne Goebel

Indexer
Erika Millen

Proofreader
San Dee Phillips

Design Manager
Sandra Schroeder

Interior Designer
Kim Scott, Bumpy Design

Compositor
Jake McFarland

Manufacturing Buyer
Dan Uhrig

Dedicated to...

Robert and Melanie Dunn
Michael and Jessica Lewis
by Bernard Lewis

Eva Lowell Churchill and Daniel Abraham Stillman
Eric Coolidge Churchill and Elka Alice Cloke
by Buntzie Ellis Churchill

Look to the neighbor before the house.
Look to the companion before the road.

—Arab proverb

Contents

Acknowledgments

It is our pleasant duty to thank a number of people who have helped in the preparation and production of this book:

Tim Moore of Pearson and Jerry Wind of Wharton, without whom there would have been no book; Lori Lyons, who helped greatly in its production, along with Anne Goebel, Jake McFarland, and San Dee Phillips.

Zainab Al-Suwaij of the American Islamic Congress, for her help and advice.

And, as always, Annamarie Cerminaro and Marci Laidler, for their patient nursing of the manuscript.

About the Authors

Bernard Lewis is Cleveland E. Dodge Professor of Near Eastern Studies, Emeritus, at Princeton University. He is the author of the best-sellers *What Went Wrong: Western Impact and Middle Eastern Response* and *The Crisis of Islam: Holy War and Unholy Terror*. He has performed the invaluable service of placing current events in the context of history. Lewis has advised policymakers in the U.S., U.K., and the Middle East on the complex relationship between Islam and the West.

A number of his articles have been extraordinarily prescient. *The Return of Islam* was published 3 years before the Iranian revolution, and the award-winning *The Roots of Muslim Rage* anticipated 9/11 by a decade. His two dozen books have been translated into more than two dozen languages, including Arabic, Persian, Turkish, and Indonesian.

His contribution to the understanding of history has been recognized by the 15 universities that have awarded him honorary doctorates.

Buntzie Ellis Churchill served for 23 years as the President of the World Affairs Council of Philadelphia, hosting dozens of world leaders from Mikhail Gorbachev and Margaret Thatcher to Henry Kissinger and Colin Powell. A member of the Council on Foreign Relations, she has served as a trustee of many non-profit organizations, including the Pennsylvania Institute of Technology and Drexel University. She has been awarded several honorary doctorates.

For a decade she hosted "WorldViews," a daily radio show, interviewing experts on international issues.

Preface

More than three hundred years ago, in 1689, the great English philosopher John Locke published *A Letter Concerning Toleration,* in which he argued that "neither Pagan, nor Mahometan, nor Jew, ought to be excluded from the civil rights of the commonwealth because of religion." In this, he gave a classical formulation of an idea which helped to inspire both the French and American revolutions, and has become an essential guiding principle of the free world. This idea, sometimes called secularism, means that religion is a private and personal matter, outside the realm of government; that membership of the political community, and the rights that go with it, belong to all citizens, of any religion or of none.

Religion remains, however, an immensely powerful factor in human affairs, with profound influence on almost every aspect of public and private, social and economic, cultural and even artistic life. No study of society, whether directed by historians at the past, by social scientists at the present, or by either at the future, can afford to disregard the religious factor. To neglect or even to underrate that factor can lead to serious misunderstandings and open the way to dangerous consequences. A French statesman once said that war is too important to be left to the generals. One might also argue that religion is too important to leave to the theologians.

There are many ways of studying religion, besides that of the theologians. Some study it as an art-historian studies paintings; others, as a bacteriologist studies bacteria. We are committed to no specific ideology or method, beyond that of dispassionate scholarship, which sees religion as a strand, or group of strands, among others, in the intricate pattern of human life. Such a study, in context, of the religious factor in human affairs is indispensable to understanding. In the Christian, or as some nowadays call it, the post-Christian world, religion has become, to a large extent, a personal and private matter. In the world of Islam, now in the early fifteenth century of its era, religion retains its centrality and remains a major force in public life, a basic theme of identity and therefore of loyalty.

For any sort of dealings with the Muslim world, some understanding, and therefore some knowledge, of Islam is essential. Unfortunately, this is rarely available and the more common perception is based on ignorance, sometimes varied by prejudice. This is particularly dangerous at a time when the Islamic world itself is undergoing major internal struggles, the outcome of which is still far from clear. It is our hope that the following pages may provide some knowledge, and thus some understanding, of one of the world's great religions—of its glorious past, its tumultuous present, and its bitterly contested future.

Introduction

The Koran is the Muslim Bible. The mosque is the Muslim church. The mullah is the Muslim priest. Friday is the Muslim Sabbath. All these statements are true; all of them can be dangerously misleading. They reflect the resemblances, even the kinship, between the Christian and Muslim worlds—the many-faceted affinity between these two religions and the religiously defined civilizations to which they gave rise, which makes such comparisons plausible and, in some measure, accurate. But at the same time, they conceal or obscure the real and sometimes profound differences between them.

It is customary to speak of the great dividing line in human civilization, even human history, as that separating the West from the rest, the Occident from the Orient. This is indeed an important dividing line—the frontier between Europe and its daughters, predominantly Christian, and the civilizations of the East, including Islam and the religions of south and east Asia. But looking at these relationships in global terms, in a broader context of time and space, there is a more important division—not on the western but on the eastern limits of the Islamic world, between the lands of Islam and the civilizations of further Asia. Compared with that division, the differences between Islam and Christendom, important though they may be, are internal differences within the same family, with common roots in Greco-Roman civilization, Judeo-Christian religion, and, beyond them, the remoter civilizations of the ancient Middle East. Even during the worst periods of conflict, dialogue was always possible, if only to quarrel. When Christians and Muslims denounced each other as infidels and threatened each other with hellfire, each understood exactly what the other meant, because they meant the same thing. Such dialogue would have been meaningless between either a Christian or a Muslim on one side and either a Hindu or a Buddhist on the other.

1

Judaism, Christianity, and Islam, sometimes referred to as "the Abrahamic religions," are closely related. All arose in the same area, where each drew on its predecessors; all three share many important doctrines and attitudes that mark them off from the other religions of the world. These religions may be grouped in various ways. We speak nowadays of the "Judeo-Christian tradition"—an old reality, but a new expression, which in earlier times would probably have been equally resented on both sides of the hyphen. Judaism and Christianity have a great deal in common, notably the Hebrew Bible, which for Christians is the Old Testament, with all the religious and ethical doctrines and traditions that it contains. A familiar example is the fatherhood of God, which Islam rejects as blasphemy. Despite this, there are a number of significant respects in which Judaism and Islam are closer to each other than either is to Christianity. Foremost among these is the belief in a divine law that meticulously regulates every aspect of life. An important part of this is the shared Jewish and Muslim preoccupation with permitted and forbidden foods. The regulations are not identical, but the underlying meaning of the Jewish Kosher and the Muslim Halal is much the same, and both emphasize the rejection of pig meat in all its forms. When the first Muslim students were sent by their governments to Europe in the early 19th century, they were told by their religious preceptors that they might eat Jewish food—but not Christian food. The Jews, it was said, observe similar though not identical rules regarding food; Christians will eat and drink anything.

Another respect in which Judaism and Islam differ from Christianity is on the question of pacifism. In the course of history, Christians made war no less frequently and no less vigorously than did other peoples and followers of other religions, but the pacifist message of the Gospels, though rarely followed, is clear. There is no such message in the Koran, and only a Messianic promise in the Old Testament.

In one very important respect, Christianity and Islam resemble each other and differ from Judaism. For both Christians and Muslims, their truths are not only universal but also exclusive and final, and it is their sacred duty not to keep them selfishly for themselves, like the Jews or the Hindus, but to bring them to all mankind, overcoming and removing or destroying whatever obstacles may be in the way (see pp. 54-55, 76, 148-149).

There are also profound and significant differences between Christianity and Islam, and these have increased in profundity and significance as a result of the changes in both worlds and in the relationship between them in modern times. Many of the traditional resemblances have become more apparent than real, and the resulting misconceptions are further complicated by the use of related or, at times, identical terms, with similar denotations but vastly different connotations. A striking example is the concept of martyrdom, deeply rooted in both Christianity and Islam but with very different meanings (see p. 214). A similar, parallel difference may be seen between the notions of the "city" in the two civilizations (see p. 106).

The problem of misconceptions resulting from different interpretations is made worse by the often superficial Westernization of institutions in modern times and, therefore, of the terms used to denote them in much of the Muslim world. This new vocabulary includes such previously unfamiliar but now widely used terms as constitution, election, president, and parliament. The resulting mutual misconceptions cover the whole range of political, economic, social, and cultural life. A frequent source of misunderstanding is in the field of values and of the standards and judgments to which they give rise. All too often, the merits of one value system are the defects of another. A few examples may suffice: Thrift equals avarice; generosity equals extravagance; courtesy equals subservience; loyalty equals nepotism and corruption. This last example is particularly significant in political and economic life. In many Muslim countries, tribalism is still a powerfulfactor, surviving in rural and urban societies in the form of the *hamula* (see p. 194). A hamula is a group of descendants from a common ancestor, usually from five to seven generations, living side by side in a rural or even urban area. According to traditional Islamic values, loyalty to one's kin is a basic moral obligation, and anyone who attains a position of power and influence, and does not use that position to benefit his kin, is failing in his social and moral duties. In the Western scale of values, this is called nepotism and/or corruption.

It is difficult to generalize about Islam. In reference to the past, the term "Islam" denotes a history of more than fourteen centuries, and to the present, a billion and a third people divided into 56 sovereign states, as well as large and growing minorities living under non-Muslim governments in Asia, Africa, Europe, and now, increasingly, the Americas.

An important and distinctive feature of the Muslim world is the extent to which religion is still seen as defining identity and, therefore, loyalty. An interesting and obvious example can be seen in the arena of international relations. At the United Nations, there is a Muslim bloc, which is a bloc of sovereign states that identify themselves by their adherence to the religion of Islam, known as the Organization of the Islamic Conference (see p. 208). In this, Muslims are unique. The Buddhist nations do not constitute a Buddhist bloc, nor do the adherents of various Christian churches form a Catholic, Orthodox, or Protestant bloc.

Christians and Muslims have much in common—a shared historical and cultural background in the Middle East; shared perceptions and beliefs, notably monotheism, prophecy, and revelation; and perhaps most important of all, the shared conviction that they are the fortunate recipients of God's final message to mankind.

In speaking of the Christian world, we use two different words: "Christianity" and "Christendom," the one denoting a religion, that is to say a system of belief and worship, the other a whole civilization that grew up under the aegis of that religion, but containing many elements not part of the religion, some even contrary to the religion. In speaking of Islam, we use the same word, "Islam," in both senses, and this gives rise to confusion, among Muslims and others. This distinction in usage extends to many areas. The term "Christian art" would be understood, by Christians and others, to refer only to votive art, connected with worship. The term "Islamic art" is used to cover the whole range of artistic creativity in the Islamic world. Similarly, it is customary to speak of Islamic mathematics, Islamic astronomy, etc., to denote the achievements of Islamic civilization in these fields. To use the word "Christian" or for that matter "Jewish" in this way would be meaningless. This difference in usage can cause dangerous misunderstandings. No one could seriously assert that Hitler and the Nazis came out of Christianity; no one can seriously deny that they came out of Christendom. This is an important distinction, which is lost in much of the current discourse about movements which arise in the Muslim world and among Muslims elsewhere, but can only be described as "Islamic" in a civilizational, not in any meaningful religious sense.

The differences between the Islamic and the Christian worlds are, of course, more than merely verbal. There are other differences, arising from the contrasting circumstances of their origins and early history. Jesus was crucified, and his followers were a persecuted minority for centuries before they obtained control of the state and were able to exercise authority. The life of Muhammad, the founder of Islam, was very different. Not he but his enemies were put to death, and during his lifetime he established a state of which he was sovereign. In Christendom, God and emperor, state and church, were distinct—sometimes in harmony, sometimes in conflict, sometimes joined, sometimes separate, sometimes one dominant, sometimes the other, but always two. In Islam, the prophet who brought the holy book and founded the faith also founded and headed the first Muslim state, and both promulgated and enforced the one all-embracing holy law. There is therefore an interpenetration of religion and politics, affecting government and law, identity and loyalty, to a degree without parallel in Judeo-Christian history.

Among Christians, the great religious wars and persecutions of the 16th and 17th centuries in time led most Christian countries to accept—in fact, if not always in law—the principle of a separation between government and religion, with a double purpose; to prevent governments from interfering in religion and to prevent religious leaders from using the coercive power of government to impose their doctrines and practices on others. In the past, this was not a problem in Islam, and Muslims saw the separation of church and state as a Christian remedy for a Christian disease, of no relevance or interest to them. Today, increasing numbers of Muslims are beginning to wonder whether they have contracted that Christian disease and might, therefore, benefit from the Christian remedy.

CHAPTER 1

The Faith and the Faithful

Since the days of the Prophet Muhammad in the early 7th century of the Common Era (CE), Muslims have had no doubt or ambiguity concerning the name of their religion and the correct designation of those who follow it. The faith is called Islam; those who follow it are called Muslims. The two words derive from the same root. The term Musulman, variously spelled, is derived from Muslim. It is widely used among non-Arab Muslims, but not in Arabic.

But what does it mean? We are often told nowadays, sometimes in all honesty, that Islam means peace. Like so many other things being said about Islam at the present time, this statement contains an element of truth, but no more than that.

A word or two about the Arabic language may help us to avoid misunderstanding. Arabic is one of a group of languages known as Semitic; the others include Hebrew, Aramaic, Ethiopic, and some of the remoter languages of Middle Eastern antiquity, such as Babylonian and Assyrian.

As in other Semitic languages, the Arabic vocabulary consists primarily of words derived from a number of three-letter roots, which can be vocalized, adjusted, and extended in various ways, to produce a large and varied vocabulary. Thus, for example, from the three-letter root *k-t-b*, with the basic meaning of "writing," we get *katab*, "write"; *kitab*, "book"; *katib*, "writer"; *kitaba*, "inscription"; *maktab*, "office" or "school," that is, a place where one writes; *maktaba*, "library" or "bookstore"; *maktub,* literally "written," which according to context may mean a "letter" or "predestined." Modern usage has added many more, including *miktab*, "typewriter," and *mukatib*, "newspaper correspondent."

The root *s-l-m*, from which the word Islam is derived, means "safe and unharmed, unimpaired." Its derivatives include words meaning both "peace" and "surrender." The best-known derivative from this root is the noun *Salam*, sometimes transcribed as *Salaam*. The word is usually translated "peace," in various senses of that word, and is sometimes used as a salutation or greeting. *Salam* or *salam 'alaikum*, "peace" or "peace be upon you," is a common form of greeting between Muslims. In the form *'alaihi's-salam* "upon him be peace," it is also used when speaking of the dead. It is rarely used in the context of peace and war, but rather in the sense of tranquility, safety, and surrender (see also pp. 149-150). It is the latter meaning that is uppermost in the use of the term Islam, meaning "to surrender oneself, to commit or resign oneself to the will of God." Islam is the act or state of submission; Muslim is the one who submits. It is in this sense, of total surrender to the will of God, that the terms Islam and Muslim have always been understood in the Islamic lands and communities.

For a long time, the outside world, more specifically, the Christian world, showed a curious reluctance to recognize or even to use the name, Islam. As successive waves of Islamic invasion brought the new faith into the formerly Christian lands of the Middle East and North Africa, and from there into Europe—first the Arabs in Spain, from their first landing in 710 CE to their final expulsion in 1492 CE, reaching across the Pyrenees even into France; then the Turks in the Balkans, reaching as far as Vienna, first in 1529 and again in 1683—the European Christians rarely, if ever, referred to these invaders by a religious designation. Instead, they called them by ethnic names, using the name of the dominant group among the invaders whom they confronted. Thus, we find the Muslim invaders of Christendom referred to, at various times and places, as Saracens, Moors, Turks, and Tatars. In time, some of these ethnic names acquired a religious connotation. Thus, in 16th century England, a convert to Islam was said to have "turned Turk," even if the conversion took place in Arabia or Persia. If the context required some explicitly religious designation, the most usual were infidel and unbeliever.

When finally, European Christians reluctantly were compelled to recognize the fact that what they confronted was not a series of barbarian invasions but a rival world religion, they invented the terms Mohammedan and Mohammedanism in the belief that Muslims worshipped Muhammad as Christians worship Christ. This is, of course, entirely false, and these terms have not been and are not used among Muslims. It is only in comparatively modern times that the terms Islam and Muslim have passed into common usage in the Christian worlds.

It may be noted in passing that Muslims have shown a similar astigmatism in their perceptions of Christianity. For a long time, and to some extent, at the present day, they, too, preferred to designate their enemies in the Holy Wars by ethnic terms—Greeks, Romans, Franks, and Slavs. Often, like their Christian opponents, they referred to them simply as unbelievers or infidels—in Arabic, *kafir*. When a specific religious designation was required, the most usual was *Nasrani*, from the Arabic name for Nazareth. The implications of this designation are obvious. It is only in comparatively recent times that the term "Christian" has been literally translated into Arabic and other Islamic languages. The Arabic term is *masihi*, from *masih*, the equivalent of the Hebrew *messiah* and the Greek *Christos*, all meaning "anointed."

This interpenetration of religious and ethnic identity has survived into modern times and may be found among both Muslims and Christians, at least in the areas where the two intermingle. A good example is the agreement of 1923 between the governments of Greece and Turkey, a compulsory exchange of minorities between the two countries. What happened is usually described in the history books as an exchange of Greeks and Turks—members of the Greek minority in Turkey were sent to Greece; members of the Turkish minority in Greece were sent to Turkey. But this description does not correspond either to the terms of the agreement or to the realities of what happened. The text of the Protocol signed in Lausanne by both governments defines the groups to be exchanged as "Turkish subjects of the Greek Orthodox religion residing in Turkey" and "Greek subjects of the Muslim religion resid-ing in Greece," and this is, in fact, what happened. Many of the so-called Greeks sent from Turkey to Greece were native Turkish speakers but Christians by religion. Similarly, many of the so-called Turks sent from Greece to Turkey were native Greek speakers who knew little or no Turkish but professed the Muslim faith. What was accomplished was not the repatriation of two ethnic minorities but the deportation of two religious minorities.

In the past, Muslim populations came under Christian rule only by conquest. In the early days—for example, in the time of the Crusades and of the Christian reconquest in Spain—many Muslim jurists and theologians held that if they had the misfortune to be conquered by infidels, Muslims were obliged—even if not forced—to emigrate to a Muslim country, since it was not possible to live a true Muslim life under an infidel government. In God's good time, they or their descen-dants would return as part of the Islamic reconquest.

With the continuing Christian reconquest first in southwestern Europe, then in southeastern Europe, followed by the expansion of Europe into the Muslim world, nowadays known as imperialism, this doctrine of emigration became impossible, and Muslim jurists and theologians adapted their rulings to a situation in which Muslims had to live under non-Muslim rule and accommodate as best they could. The question that never seems to have entered their minds was that Muslims would voluntarily emigrate to non-Muslim countries.

This is a new reality, for Muslims even more than for their new hosts, and raises a whole series of interesting issues. The basic question is—is one a member of a religion subdivided into nationalities or of a nation subdivided into religions? The answer to this question may determine allegiance and much more.

Muslims settling in Western countries get both more and less than they expect and see as their right. By residence, naturalization, and, in the second generation, by birth, they acquire rights of expression and participation which are virtually unknown in all but a few of the countries of the Muslim world. On the other hand, what they want—and do not get—is a right that was in the past accorded as a matter of course to the non-Muslim minorities under most Muslim governments: the right to conduct their own communal affairs (see pp. 56, 188). This is, of course, not possible in modern Western countries, where jurisdiction is always defined by territory, not by community, and where law is secular, not religious.

CHAPTER 2

The Pillars of the Faith

For Muslims, the definition of Islam and acceptance as a member of the Muslim community rests on what are known as "the five pillars," five basic obligations. They are

The creed or declaration of the faith
Prayer
Charity
Fasting
Pilgrimage

The Creed

The basic creed, acceptance or rejection of which marks the difference between the Muslim and the unbeliever, consists of two clear, unambiguous sentences: "I testify that there is no God but Allah. I testify that Muhammad is the Prophet of Allah."

The first of these is an affirmation of monotheism, and a rejection—in earlier times of polytheism and idolatry, in modern times of agnosticism and atheism. The second affirms the mission of Muhammad, not just as God's prophet but as his final prophet to mankind, after whom there will be no other.

Prayer

There are two terms for prayer in Islamic usage. The first, *salat*, refers to ritual prayers in a prescribed form and at prescribed times; the second, *du'a*, denotes a personal prayer or invocation addressed by the believer to God.

Salat comes in a set formula and must be recited five times a day at specific times: dawn, midday, early afternoon, sunset, and evening. The form of worship and postures or movements of the worshipper are elaborately regulated. The worshipper, wherever he may be in the world, must face in the direction of the Ka'ba (see p. 199) in Mecca, the birthplace of the Prophet, the first home of the Muslim revelation and of Islam itself.

The actual prayer consists of passages from the Koran. There are no hymns, in the Christian or Jewish sense of that word. Music and poetry form a rich heritage in Islamic culture, including Islamic piety and devotion, notably, though not exclusively, among the mystics. But they have no place in the daily and weekly prayer.

People praying in a parking lot near an overflowing mosque.
(iStockphoto)

In addition to the five daily prayers, which the believer must perform wherever he may be, there are other prescribed ritual prayers. The most important are the Friday prayer, performed at midday in the mosque, and the prayers of the two holy days of fasting and sacrifice (see *'id,*

p. 197). There are other prayers which depend on circumstances, such as the prayer for rain, at an eclipse, and over the dead.

Women praying.
(Copyright Abbas /Magnum Photos)

The *du'a* is nonformulaic. It may be offered at any time, in any place that is not ritually impure (see Chapter 4, "The Mosque"). It is, essentially, a specific appeal or invocation to God, for oneself, for another, or against another. It may, thus, be a blessing or a curse. The worshipper may choose his own words, but traditional texts and prayers exist and may be used. Often, the *du'a* is an expression of religious devotion, even passion, and the practice has given rise to some truly remarkable mystical poetry. It may also be used in prayers for the state, ruler, community, family, or other entities.

The Muslim Friday is the equivalent of the Jewish Saturday and the Christian Sunday, in the sense that it is the day of public and communal prayer, when the faithful gather in their place of worship and pray together before the Lord. It is also traditionally honored by serving special dishes and wearing better clothes. There is, however, a certain difference. For Jews and Christians, the Sabbath is a day of rest, important enough to constitute one of the Ten Commandments. For Muslims, it is primarily a day of public prayer rather than of rest; indeed, it was often a day of heightened economic activity in the markets. There are some references in early times to Muslims resting on Friday, even a condemnation by a jurist of those who imitate this Jewish and Christian practice. But it came to be increasingly accepted, and a weekly day of rest, usually but not everywhere Friday, is now observed in most Muslim countries. It is not, like the Jewish Sabbath, imposed and regulated by the holy law. In the Western world, the Sabbath grew into the weekend, with its obvious attractions and advantages. At the present time, this practice is becoming more widely accepted in the Islamic world.

Charity

The third pillar is known in Arabic as *zakat*, which is variously translated as "alms-giving" and "alms-tax." From the earliest times, it seems to have been conceived as a tax paid by Muslims to the community, the proceeds of which were to be used for the relief of the needy. It has been described, not inaccurately, as an early form of social security. By the Middle Ages, it had already developed into a vast and complex system of charitable foundations and institutions all over the world of Islam, providing a wide range of services (see Chapter 10, "Islam and the Economy.")

Fasting

Fasting refers primarily to the fast of the month of Ramadan, during which the believers are required to fast from dawn until dusk for the whole month. The rules concerning the fast are laid down in the Koran (2:179–181 and 183). These rules are amplified by the traditions and by the jurists. Muslims must abstain from all kinds of food and drink, from tobacco, sexual relations, and even perfume. Since the Muslim year is purely lunar (see pp. 176-177), the fasting month of Ramadan is not tied to any particular season but rotates throughout the entire solar calendar. When Ramadan occurs during the summer, the long days make the fasting particularly difficult. The story is told of some

Muslim seamen on a British merchant vessel in the 18th century who found themselves in the Arctic Circle, not previously known to the Muslims, during the month of Ramadan. Despite the entreaties of their shipmates, they waited for the sunset that never came and starved to death.

The obligation of fasting may be remitted in certain circumstances: for the underage, the sick, the elderly, the traveler, a woman in menstruation or childbirth, or a fighter in a holy war. In addition to the fast of Ramadan, fasting for longer or shorter periods may be required or offered as atonement for some offense. A married woman may undertake a voluntary fast only with the permission of her husband. Breaking a voluntary fast incurs no penalty.

For most Muslims, the beginning and end of a day of fasting are determined by observation. The fast ends, traditionally, when one can no longer distinguish between a white thread and a black thread. For some groups, such as the Isma'ilis (see pp. 63-64), the time is determined by calculating the moment of sunset, and, in the past, this sometimes led to quarrels and clashes when one group noisily celebrated the ending of the fast while others were still enduring its hardships.

Pilgrimage

The Arabic term, also used in other Islamic languages, for the annual pilgrimage to Mecca is *Hajj*. The same word is used in a slightly modified form as a title for those who have performed the pilgrimage. They may indicate this by wearing a green band around their headgear. For Christians, pilgrimage to the holy places of their religion is, so to speak, an optional extra and may be performed at any time that is convenient. For Muslims, it is one of the five basic obligations of the faith and is incumbent on every Muslim who can afford it at least once in a lifetime. It is an act of piety to visit the holy cities at any time, but the formal pilgrimage takes place at a fixed time the first half of the last month of the Muslim year, known as Dhu'l-Hijja. This, too, is determined by the purely lunar Muslim calendar and rotates throughout the solar year.

The pilgrimage in the holy cities of Mecca and Medina involves a series of rituals and observances, usually with the participation of great numbers of pilgrims. Non-Muslims are not permitted to be present or to set foot at any time in the holy cities or, more generally, in the Hejaz (correctly Hijaz) in the northwestern part of the Arabian peninsula. The solitary exception is the seaport of Jedda, where foreign merchants, consuls, contractors, and others are allowed to visit and, with certain restrictions, to reside. In addition to the great pilgrimage, there is also the "little pilgrimage" or 'umra, which is a personal choice rather than a communal obligation.

The pilgrimage has had an enormous impact on Islam, from medieval times until the present day. Every year, it brings great numbers of Muslims from every part of the vast Muslim world and beyond, of widely differing national, ethnic, social, and cultural backgrounds, to travel, often over vast distances, and join with others in a common sequence of ritual and worship. These journeys are not like the mindless, collective migrations familiar in premodern history. They are, for most pilgrims, a voluntary choice and give rise to a wide range of personal experience.

For two kinds of pilgrims in particular, the scholar and the merchant, these experiences, and the knowledge and contacts that they brought, could be of immense importance. The pilgrimage has been, and still is, an effective means of universal communication, and, therefore, of common awareness and identity, without parallel in the premodern world. It was also immensely valuable to the rulers of the holy cities of the time, both for acquiring information and for exercising influence.

The control of the holy cities and, with it, of the annual pilgrimage was often fiercely contested between rival Muslim monarchs. It was customary for the ruler or suzerain of the Hijaz to use the title Khadim al-Haramayn, the servant of the two holy places. Since 1926, this privilege has belonged to the royal house of Saud.

View of the Ka'ba in the courtyard of the main mosque, Mecca, Saudi Arabia.
(©Mecca, Saudi Arabia/ Bildarchiv Steffens/ The Bridgeman Art Library)

Most religions divide possible human actions into three categories: commanded, permitted, forbidden. The Islamic classification is more complex and has five categories: commanded, recommended, permitted, disapproved, forbidden.

Islamic civilization, like some though by no means all others, has its own vein of humor. What is perhaps distinctive about Islamic humor is its centrality and antiquity. Muslims have been telling jokes about themselves and about their sanctities since the advent of Islam in the 7th century. More remarkably, this rich vein of humor is amply documented in the classical, literary, and even religious works in Arabic, Persian, Turkish, and no doubt other languages of the Islamic world. Examples of humor are found throughout this book.

ISLAMIC HUMOR

An old Turkish anecdote illustrates and caricatures the complaints of the dervishes about Muslim society, and the suspicions of Muslim society about the dervishes. The story tells that a dervish went one day to the house of a rich man to ask for alms. The rich man, doubtful of the dervish's piety, asked him to enumerate the five pillars of Islam.

The dervish responded by reciting the declaration of faith: "I testify that there is no God but Allah; I testify that Muhammad is the Apostle of Allah," and then was silent.

"And what about the rest?" asked the rich man. "What about the other four?"

To this the dervish replied, "You rich men have abandoned pilgrimage and charity, and we poor dervishes have abandoned prayer and fasting, so what remains but the unity of God and the apostolate of Muhammad?"

Of the Ten Commandments set forth in Exodus, three, banning polytheism, idolatry, and blasphemy, are concerned with man's duty to God; one, imposing the Sabbath as a day of worship and also as a day of rest for all, deals with duties both toward God and toward one's fellow men. The remaining six are concerned exclusively with human relations.

In contrast, of the five Muslim pillars of the faith, four are concerned with belief and worship and only the fifth with one's fellow men. The remaining prohibitions (murder, theft, adultery, and perjury) are dealt with elsewhere in the Koran and the Traditions, and at greater length in the treatises on the Holy Law. Among the Shi'a, there are additional basic principles, notably two derived from the Koran—to command what is right and forbid what is evil. For Sunnis, too, though they do not figure among the pillars of the faith, these two Koranic injunctions are of profound importance. All religions, in one way or another, instruct the believers to do good and refrain from evil. For Muslims, that is not enough; it is their duty actively to command good and forbid evil. (For Muslim rules regarding food and drink, see the Appendix, "Some Practical Matters.")

≈

At the time of the advent of Islam in the 7th century, most inhabitants of the Arabian peninsula, where the Prophet Muhammad was born, lived and died, and founded the first Islamic community, still worshipped many gods. The only exceptions were small communities of Jews and Christians in various parts of the peninsula, formed partly by migration, partly by conversion. The countries that became the heartlands of Islam, nowadays known as the Middle East, were still divided between the two rival empires, Persia and Byzantium. The empire of Persia consisted of the plateau of Iran and most of the country now called Iraq. The dominant and official religion was the faith of Zoroaster, which still survives among small minorities in Iran and in the Indian subcontinent, to which many Zoroastrians migrated after the Arab/Islamic conquest of their homeland. Byzantium is the name that modern scholarship has given to the Christianized East Roman Empire, and, more specifically, to the great city of Constantinople, now known as Istanbul. It was dedicated as his capital by the first Christian Emperor, Constantine, in 330 CE.

In Iraq, even under Persian rule, Christians and Jews formed a significant element in the population. To the west of Iraq, in the vast lands of the Byzantine Empire, the dominant and majority religion was Christianity. At that time, the world of Christendom included the entire Mediterranean and all of what is now Turkey, Syria, Lebanon, Jordan, Israel, the Palestine territories, Egypt, and North Africa. As in Iraq, many of these lands included significant Jewish minorities. For Jews and, with one exception that we shall look at in a moment, for

Christians, the attestation of the unity of God was no problem. More difficult was the second clause of the creed: the attestation that Muhammad is the Prophet of God and, as a corollary, that the book he brought is an authentic divine revelation and the immutable word of God.

Although not explicitly stated in the creed, the belief was soon generally adopted by Muslims that Muhammad was not only a prophet; he was also the last of a series of prophets, and after him there would be no other. There are numerous references in the Koran and the traditions to Muhammad's predecessors in the prophetic mission, a number of divinely appointed apostles and prophets who, at different times and in different places, brought God's message of truth. These include many familiar figures from both the Old and New Testaments, as well as some from Arabian history, all seen in the Muslim perception as paving the way for Muhammad's advent and mission. The earliest revelation, given to Ibrahim (Abraham), is lost. The books of revelation for three subsequent prophets still exist, though not in their original and authentic form: the *zubur* of David, the *tawrat* of Moses, and the *injil* of Jesus. The first of these clearly means "the Psalms." The second is the Torah, the Jewish name for the first five books of the Bible, the five books of Moses. The *injil* is the *evangelion*, the Greek term for the Gospels.

In many ways, this respect, indeed veneration, of Jewish and Christian sanctities and scriptures might have facilitated the acceptance by Jews and Christians of this new and final revelation. But a difficulty arose. The Koranic versions of Biblical figures and events occasionally differ, sometimes markedly, from those portrayed in the Old and New Testaments. For Jews and Christians, the explanation was simple: Muhammad or his informants got it wrong. For Muslims, this explanation was at once blasphemous and absurd. God's Prophet does not get it wrong; God is not misinformed. If the Koranic version of Biblical events differed from that presented in the Bible, there could be only one acceptable explanation: The Jews and Christians had proved unworthy custodians of the revelations entrusted to them and had allowed the sacred texts to be corrupted and distorted. In the Muslim view, it was this distortion that made a new and final revelation necessary.

Here, another marked distinction must be noted. The advent of Christianity brought a New Testament, to be added to the Jewish Bible, henceforth renamed the Old Testament, but still part of the holy book for Christians. The Koran is not a third testament to be added to the other two. It is a complete revelation, and it supplants and replaces its distorted predecessors. The Jews and Christians are accused, specifically, of having removed passages from the Bible predicting the advent of Muhammad. More seriously, the Christians are accused of introducing new doctrines that verge on polytheism. The reference, of course, is to the divinity of Christ and to the Holy Trinity. The Koran (5:119) quotes God as saying: "O, Jesus, Son of Mary, did you tell people: 'Worship me and my mother as gods apart from God'?" To which, of course, Jesus replies with an emphatic and unequivocal denial. Another passage (112) is more explicit: "He is God, one, eternal. He does not beget, nor is he begotten"—a clear and explicit challenge to one of the basic beliefs of Christianity. Significantly, the same verse appears among the inscriptions on the Dome of the Rock, which the caliph Abd al-Malik built in Jerusalem in 691-692 CE, and on the gold coinage struck by the caliph at about the same time.

The challenge to Christendom and to the Christian world role was many-faceted. The striking of gold coins had, until that time, been an exclusive privilege of the Roman emperors and later of the Christian Byzantine emperors of Constantinople. The Dome of the Rock was located at the Temple Mount, a place of sanctity for Christians and Jews. The message was clear: Your religion and, with it, your empire are superseded. We are taking over.

In addition to the basic theological creed concerning deity, prophecy, and revelation, Islam, like its precursors Judaism and Christianity, offers the believer some detailed information concerning the hereafter: the survival of the soul, the resurrection, the final struggle, the Day of Judgment, punishment in hell or reward in heaven. Heaven is called *janna*, an Arabic word meaning "garden" or "paradise." Hell is known as *jahannum* (or Gehenna in the Bible) or simply as *al-Nar*, "the fire." Hell is the abode of the Devil, known as Shaytan (Satan) or Iblis (Diabolos);

paradise is the place of God and his angels. Muslim accounts of the final struggle do not differ greatly from those of Jews and Christians, with Dajjal as the evil equivalent of anti-Christ or Gog and Magog, and with the forces of good led by the Mahdi, the divinely-guided one, who will lead them to their final victory, sending the resurrected souls to their eternal destinations in heaven or hell. All this follows more or less the same pattern as the two previous religions. Unlike the Jewish paradise, which accepts "the righteous of all the peoples of the world," the Muslim paradise, like the Christian paradise, admits only the true believers, that is, Christians in the one case, Muslims in the other. Their hells are more or less the same, but their heavens are somewhat differently appointed. They are described in some detail in the Koran, and in much greater detail in the traditions and commentaries. (See "hell" and "paradise," pp. 195, 198, 209.)

CHAPTER 3

Scripture, Tradition, and Law

The Koran is the Muslim "Bible" in the sense that it is revered as a holy book of revelation, containing God's guidance to humanity. But it differs from the Bible—both the Old and New Testaments—in several significant respects. The Bible is not a single book. It is a collection of different books, by different authors, written or revealed at different times, over a period of many centuries. The Old Testament is in Hebrew, with the exception of some passages that are in Aramaic. The New Testament is in Greek, although, according to some scholars, certain passages may be translated from an earlier original in Aramaic. For Muslims, the Koran is a single book, revealed to a single prophet. It is not just divinely inspired; it is, in the most literal sense, divine. In early Islamic times, a theological controversy arose among Muslims as to whether the Koran was created by God at the time of its revelation to Muhammad or had existed since all eternity. The prevailing view, since then generally accepted among Muslims, is that the Koran is eternal and uncreated, coexisting with God since all eternity.

Because of the divine sanctity of the text, translation from the Arabic original into other languages is in principle forbidden. The task of translation is, in any case, deemed impossible because of the divinely miraculous beauty of its language. As Islam was adopted by ever greater numbers of non-Arabs, speaking a wide variety of languages other than Arabic, versions of the Koran in these languages were in fact prepared. But they were presented as commentaries and explanations rather than as translations, and none of them attained the sacred status accorded to some translations of the Bible among Christians and, to a lesser extent, Jews—such as the Latin Vulgate, the King James Bible in English, and a number of translations into the languages used by the Eastern churches. Some of these are accorded a sacred status, not less than that of the Greek and Hebrew originals. There is nothing comparable among Muslims for whom, whatever their native language, the Arabic text of the Koran alone is divine and authoritative. The fact that the language of the Koran is Arabic is mentioned and, indeed, stressed in many places.[1]

The Koran is the primary source of Muslim doctrine, law, and practice. But it is not the only one. At an early date, Muslims adopted the principle that the Prophet, in addition to bringing and promulgating the divine Koran, was himself divinely inspired in all that he said and did, and that his actions and utterances could therefore be cited to clarify, elaborate, and where necessary, even supplement the Koran. This rapidly became an important additional source of guidance for Muslims. The very rapid growth and expansion of the Muslim community, and of the state which it founded, confronted the Muslims with a series of problems and issues, notably in the fields of government and then of empire, for which the Koran provided no explicit guidance, and the precedents of the Prophet, as preserved by tradition, acquired major importance.

During the Prophet's lifetime and immediately after, there was no written record of his words and deeds. Instead, they were orally transmitted, and it was not until later that they were collected and committed to writing.

This reliance on oral tradition inevitably raised questions concerning the accuracy and sometimes even the authenticity of such traditions. These questions were aggravated by the many internal conflicts that arose among the Muslims during the decades following the Prophet's death. In an argument between rival Muslim factions or contenders, no better evidence could be produced than a saying of the Prophet, supporting this or that idea or claimant. This inevitably led to charges of

---

[1] For example, Koran 26:195; 41:44; 12:2; 20:113; 39:28; 41:3; 42:7; 43:3.

slanting or even inventing tradition. Within a very short time hundreds of thousands of traditions were being cited.

ISLAMIC HUMOR

Someone said to Ash'ab: "Instead of wasting your time telling jokes, why don't you relate traditions [hadith] concerning the Prophet? That would be a worthier and nobler thing."

"By God," replied Ash'ab, "I have heard many traditions and related them."

"Then tell us one," said the man.

"I heard from Nafi'," said Ash'ab, "on the authority of Ibn Umar, that the Prophet of God, may God bless and save him, said: 'There are two qualities, such that whoever has them both is among God's chosen.'"

"That is a fine tradition," said the man. "What are these two qualities?"

"Nafi' forgot one and I have forgotten the other," said Ash'ab.

From the beginning, Muslim scholars were well aware of these problems and devised an elaborate science and method to cope with them. The individual tradition—the saying or action attributed to the Prophet—is called a *hadith*, an Arabic word with the connotation of "narrative." Each hadith had to be verified by an *isnad*, roughly "support," consisting of a chain of narrators attesting both the provenance and authenticity of the narrative. The classical form of the isnad was: "I heard from so-and-so, who heard from so-and-so, who heard from so-and-so, who was there, that on such-and-such an occasion, the Prophet said or did…." The early Muslim scholars developed an elaborate science for the authentication and classification of hadiths, relying partly on a critical examination of the text of the narrative, but mainly of the isnad.

The early scholars divided hadiths into three categories:

- **Sound**—Those where both the isnad and the text were impeccable.

- **Good**—Traditions that seemed generally acceptable but with some questions about the isnad.
- **Weak**—Those which may contain authentic material but are subject to some doubts over either content or isnad.

Beyond these, many other traditions were rejected entirely as fabricated or distorted. In time, early Muslim scholars compiled great collections of hadiths, which came to be accepted as authentic and binding by most Muslims.

ISLAMIC HUMOR

Another joke about hadith: Two merchants, one Muslim and one Christian, met onboard a ship and were chatting amicably. At a certain moment, the Christian merchant took a flask of wine out of his bag and said to his Muslim colleague: "I would ask you to join me in drinking some wine, but I know that it is forbidden by your religion, and I do not wish to offend you."

"How do you know that this is wine?" asked the Muslim merchant.

"I sent my slave to the market, and he bought it from a well-known Jewish wine merchant."

The Muslim merchant replied: "Sometimes we even reject traditions related on the authority of the companions of the Prophet. Do you expect me to believe a tradition related by a Christian, on the authority of his slave, on the authority of a Jewish wine merchant? Give me that flask!"

The "discovery" of new traditions to buttress one or another cause or claimant never entirely ceased; for example, a tradition was "found" and published in some Arabic newspapers in which the Prophet predicted and approved Saddam Hussein's annexation of Kuwait in 1991. But for the overwhelming majority of what we might call serious Muslims, the task of collecting, authenticating, and classifying the traditions of the Prophet was completed in the early centuries of Islam, and the resulting collections constitute a second source of guidance, after the Koran.

The expansion of Islam, by conquest and conversion, continued at a rapid pace, and with vast new areas and populations came new and increasingly complex problems, for which neither Koran nor hadith provided explicit guidance. To confront these problems, a principle was adopted known as *ijtihad*, a term which might be translated as the exercise of independent judgment in dealing with a case or interpreting a rule of law. One who practices ijtihad is called a *mujtahid*. The practice of ijtihad is contrasted with that of *taqlid*, literally "imitation," following existing practice and tradition. There is no claim of infallibility, and it is recognized that a ruling by ijtihad may turn out to be wrong. According to a hadith of the Prophet, the mujtahid is rewarded for making the effort and venturing an opinion; if the opinion turns out to be correct, his reward is doubled.

In the early centuries of the Islamic era, ijtihad was extensively practiced by theologians and, more especially, by jurists to find acceptable Islamic solutions to the many new problems that arose. By the middle of the 9th century CE, there was a significant body of legal rulings and precedents, and the question was increasingly asked: By whom and how is ijtihad to be practiced? The prevailing opinion became restrictive, and more and more took the view that only the great scholars of early Islam had this right, and that their successors and disciples could only follow them. In approximately the 10th century CE, Sunni scholars generally agreed that all the basic questions had already been examined and resolved; henceforth, the task of jurists was to apply and, at most, to interpret the teachings that had been handed down to them. Independent reasoning in matters of holy law was no longer necessary and, therefore, no longer possible. This principle, often referred to as "the closing of the gate of ijtihad," was generally adopted by Sunni Muslims. It was rejected in principle by the Shi'a, who still claimed the right of ijtihad and took to calling their professional men of religion by the term mujtahid. But in practice, their attitudes and policies differed little from those of the Sunnis. From time to time, major Muslim scholars and thinkers appeared who indeed claimed the right of ijtihad, but they are few, and, for the most part, their influence was limited.

A notable exception was Ibn Taymiyya (died 1328), the spiritual ancestor of the Wahhabis (see pp. 157-158).

In Western thought and practice, one of the primary functions of
the state is legislation—to prepare and promulgate laws and to amend,
modify, or even on occasion repeal them, according to time and circumstance. In the classical Muslim perception, there is no human legislative function. The law is divine, eternal, and all-embracing and is
promulgated by revelation and elaborated by tradition and interpretation. The legal function of the state is to apply and enforce the divinely
given law. This law is known as the *Shari'a,* meaning "path" or more
especially, "the path to a well or spring." In principle, it includes all
aspects of public and private, communal and personal life.

Successive generations of jurists developed the holy law of Islam
into an elaborate system of jurisprudence, as well as of substantive
law. According to an early saying attributed to the Prophet, "Difference of opinion within my community is part of God's mercy;" that is,
disagreement is a permissible, even a good thing. From an early date,
different juristic schools developed, in broad agreement on essentials,
but sometimes differing quite extensively on points of detail. Among
Sunni Muslims, there are four recognized schools, each recognizing
the others as being within the permitted limits of dissent:

- **Hanafi** or **Hanafite**—Takes its name from Abu Hanifa al-
  Nu'man (circa 699–767). The Hanafi school spread from Iraq
  westward to Syria and eastward to Central Asia and India. It
  was particularly favored by the Turkic dynasties of Central Asia
  and later became the more or less official doctrine of the Ottoman Empire. It is still officially recognized in former Ottoman
  provinces, though it is followed only by dwindling minorities.
- **Maliki** or **Malikite**—Named after Malik ibn Anas (circa
  710–796). It is now and has for some time been the dominant
  Sunni school in North Africa west of Egypt, as well as in the
  Sudan. There are also significant numbers of Maliki Muslims
  in sub-Saharan West Africa. It was the dominant school in
  Moorish Spain.

- **Shafi'i** or **Shafi'ite**—Named after Abu Abdallah Muhammad al-Shafi'i (767–820). The Shafi'i school commands considerable following in southern Arabia, Egypt, east Africa, southeast Asia, and parts of central Asia.
- **Hanbali** or **Hanbalite**—Named after Ahmad ibn Hanbal (780–855). The dominant school in Saudi Arabia and in Saudi-sponsored institutions abroad. The Hanbalis take a strictly conservative line, recognizing no source of authority other than the Koran and the traditions of the Prophet. They are equally opposed to Sufi mysticism and to speculative theology. In the 18th century, in Ottoman Arabia, Hanbali doctrines and teachings inspired the founder of the Wahhabi movement.

The Shi'a had their own versions of Muslim law, agreeing with the Sunnis on most points and differing on some. Most Sunni Muslims accept them, in fact if not in theory, as a fifth school, but some, notably the Hanbalis, reject them as false.

From an early date, differences of opinion arose among Muslim jurists concerning the application of Shari'a outside the lands of Islam. According to a Sunni view, that of the Hanafi school, Shari'a law only applies and can therefore only be enforced in the "House of Islam," that is to say, in countries under Muslim rule. An eminent 11th-century jurist, using a familiar legal device, formulated an extreme case to clarify and emphasize the point. If a Muslim traveling in the lands of the unbelievers commits robbery and murder and returns with his loot to the lands of Islam, he cannot be prosecuted for the murder, nor can the property be touched, since the offense was committed outside the jurisdiction of Islam. It is for the legal authorities of the unbelievers to take action, if they are willing and able to do so. According to this view, Muslim law does not apply, and Muslim judges are not concerned with what happens outside the realm of Islam.

An exact opposite view is taken by the Shi'a and by some groups among the Sunnis. According to this, the jurisdiction of Islamic law and the authority of its judiciary apply to Muslims wherever they may be, even in the lands of the infidels. Even there, they are still bound to obey Muslim law and should be punished for violating it. Some jurists take an intermediate position, arguing that a Muslim may be tried and punished for an offense committed in the lands of the unbelievers, but only when he returns to the lands of Islam, not while he is still living in the lands of the unbelievers.

In the classical Muslim view Shari'a law prevails and must be enforced wherever Muslim governments rule—that is to say, anywhere in the House of Islam. It did not generally apply to non-Muslim subjects within the Muslim state who lived under their own laws administered by their own courts, subject of course to the general supervision of the Islamic states and authorities.

From an early date, the question arose on the legal position of Muslims living under non-Muslim rule. This problem was considered under three headings. The first was that of conversion—the case of the unbeliever in the land of the unbelievers who sees the light and embraces Islam.

The second is the case of the captive—the Muslim traveler or soldier who has the misfortune to be captured by infidels and taken to the lands of the infidels where he is held by them. In both of these cases, the jurists agreed that the Muslim must do his best as far as possible to observe the laws of Islam, and must return to an Islamic land as soon as possible.

The third case which begins to be considered with the turn of the tide—the reconquest in Spain, Portugal, and southern Italy, and the holding by the Crusaders of parts of the Levant—is that of Muslims living in countries that have passed under non-Muslim rule. Opinions among the jurists on this point differed. In the early period, the more common view was that it was their duty to leave as soon as they could and go to a Muslim country and wait there until, in God's good time, their homelands would be reconquered and they could return triumphantly under the banner of Islam.

But as the process of Christian reconquest continued and gave way in time to the imperial expansion of Christendom, this ceased to be practical, and Muslim jurists were compelled to confront the disagreeable problem: How is a Muslim to live a Muslim life under infidel rule? The question of a Muslim migrating of his own free will from the lands of Islam to the lands of unbelief never seems to have occurred to the classical jurists, nor indeed to modern jurists, until fairly recently.

On February 14, 1989 the Ayatollah Khomeini added a new dimension to this issue. On that date he issued a *fatwa*, a ruling, pronouncing a death sentence on the London-based Muslim novelist Salman Rushdie, the author of *The Satanic Verses*, "which has been compiled, printed and published in opposition to Islam, the Prophet, and the Koran." Up to this point, Khomeini's fatwa is within the limits of Shi'a jurisprudence. But in this fatwa he goes a significant step further and extends the death sentence to "all those involved in this publication who are aware of its contents," i.e. the presumably non-Muslim printers, publishers, and distributors of the book in Britain, the United States, and elsewhere. The fatwa continues: "I call on all zealous Muslims to dispatch them quickly, wherever they may be found, so that no one will dare to insult Islamic sanctities again. Anyone who is himself killed in this path will be deemed a martyr."

This would appear to be the first occasion when a Muslim jurist claimed jurisdiction over non-Muslims in a non-Muslim country. Since then, others, both Muslims and non-Muslims, have followed the same path.

More recently, there have been attempts even by non-Muslims to apply Shari'a law in the West. One example is a German judge who refused to grant a divorce decree requested by a Muslim woman on the grounds that her husband beat her. The judge's reason: While wife-beating is forbidden in German law, it is permitted in Shari'a law. (This decision was later reversed by a higher judicial authority.) Another

Muslims should not be allowed to live outside the secular laws of the countries in which they abide

example: The Archbishop of Canterbury, the highest ecclesiastical authority in Great Britain, suggested that some elements of Shariʿa be accepted and enforced for Muslim citizens of the United Kingdom. Some European governments are already giving tacit acceptance, such as in the recognition of plural wives in immigration permits, tax allowances, and welfare payments.

Some now even try to do something which was never done in the classical Islamic states, that is, to impose Shariʿa on non-Muslims in non-Muslim states. Some examples include Muslim taxi drivers who refuse to accept blind passengers with seeing-eye dogs, since dogs are regarded as unclean; or to accept airport passengers carrying duty-free liquor. (Alcohol is forbidden to Muslims but not to others; pp. 58, 178.)

A new and significant change appeared when the publication in Denmark of a series of cartoons depicting the Prophet Mohammad in a negative way aroused widespread riots and demands for the punishment of the publishers. In the past, insults to the Prophet by unbelievers in the lands of the unbelievers did not trouble Muslims. Even unbelievers under Muslim rule were rarely punished for this offense. The classical Islamic jurists were careful to point out that the tolerated subject unbeliever is not to be punished for that which constitutes his unbelief. This is known and accepted. The rejection and even abuse of the Prophet, which were normal in medieval and early modern Christian literature and art, aroused no concern or even interest.

The Western distinction between church and state is, in classic Islamic terms, meaningless. Muslim thinkers from an early date distinguished between the affairs of this world and the affairs of the next, but the distinction expressed in such pairs of terms as spiritual and temporal, lay and ecclesiastical, sacred and profane, is unknown to classical Islamic thought and practice, and indeed these terms had no equivalent in Islamic languages until comparatively modern times, when they were borrowed or invented.

The same modernity also brought the first attempts to compile and promulgate codes of law, beginning in the mid-19th century, and clearly under European influence. Before that, there was in principle no human power of legislation. One of the first descriptions of a Western legislative assembly by a Muslim visitor comes from the late 18th century and was the work of the Indian-born Persian scholar Mirza Abu Talib Khan. Between 1779 and 1803, he traveled extensively in the West. He seems to have spent most of his time in London, but he also visited Ireland and returned via France, Italy, and the Middle East. On his return home, he wrote a book describing his adventures and giving his impressions of the people and places he had visited. His initial impressions were not favorable. Speaking of the British House of Commons, he remarked: "The first time I saw this assembly, they reminded me of two flocks of Indian parakeets, sitting upon opposite mango trees, scolding at each other…." But Mirza Abu Talib Khan was not put off by this first impression: "It is not, however, to be inferred from this circumstance that parliaments are of no utility; on the contrary, they are of the greatest service. In the first place, they regulate the taxes for the year; they are a check on all contractors and public agents and restrain the Ministers within proper bounds upon every occasion." He goes on to explain to his readers the reason why the English need a parliament. "The Christians," he explains, "unlike the Muslims and the Jews, do not acknowledge having received any divine laws concerning worldly matters; instead, they take upon themselves to make such regulations as the exigencies of the times require."

In fact, in a wide, varied, and complex society, some legislative change was inevitable. It took a number of forms—the interpretation and reinterpretation of sacred texts by recognized authorities and the tabulation, by rulers or their appointed officials, of what were called rules and regulations but were often, in practice if not in theory, legislation. But the legislative function was never formally recognized until the age of Westernization, and until then, there were no formally constituted and recognized legislative bodies.

The creation of such bodies in modern times, and the legal and social changes that they produced, became a major grievance among both conservative and radical Islamists. Shariʿa is usually translated "holy law," not because it deals exclusively or even primarily with holy in the sense of religious matters, but because of its divine origin. In principle, it covers the whole range of human life and activity. It deals, of course, with religious matters such as prayer, fasting, pilgrimage, and the like; however, it also covers the whole range of what we would call constitutional law, civil law (including marriage and divorce), inheritance law, and criminal law. In the 19th and early 20th centuries, under European influence and sometimes under European pressure, several Muslim governments, notably in Turkey, Egypt, and Iran, experimented with elected Parliaments entrusted with the task, among others, of preparing legal codes. While these introduced many new ideas and practices, the principle was, in theory, maintained that this entire process, including the most radical reforms, fell within the scope of the Shari'a. Thus, for example, after the Young Turk Revolution of 1908, the purpose of which was to install constitutional government in Turkey, the Sultan's "speech from the throne," prepared for him by his ministers and read by him to Parliament, began with a reference to "constitutional government as prescribed by the Shari'a." The Young Turks were mostly secular modernists but still felt it necessary to include this acknowledgment.

More recent constitutions in Muslim countries, though more secular in tone, often include some vague references to the Shari'a. These clauses variously lay down that the Shari'a shall be "a source," "a principal source," or even "*the* principal source" of legislation. Sometimes the point is made the other way around, and the clause states that no law shall be enacted or rule followed that contravenes the Shari'a. According to an old Muslim dictum, to forbid what God permits is as bad as to permit what God forbids. In both respects, strict interpretation of the Shari'a would present serious and sometimes insurmountable barriers to modernization, notably in such matters as abolishing slavery and emancipating women.

For more than two centuries, Muslim reformers have been trying to overcome these barriers while remaining faithful to what they see as the true essence of the Shari'a. One Egyptian judge went so far as to say that Shari'a should be seen as principles of jurisprudence rather than as rules of law. His ideas, like those of other reformers, were roundly and soundly condemned by those who saw themselves as the custodians of the eternal and unchanging holy law.

CHAPTER 4

The Mosque

The name mosque comes from the Arabic *masjid*, literally "a place of prostration," that is, of worship. In this sense, as a place of prayer, the mosque is the equivalent of the church in Christendom. Until modern times, it was in no way the equivalent of the church in the other sense of that word—an institution parallel with the state, with its own hierarchy and jurisdiction, its own laws and even courts to administer them. In that sense, the church had no equivalent in classical Islam, where state and church were one, both in principle regulated by the same holy law.

In early times, in places newly added to the realms of Islam, Muslims tended to adapt or copy preexisting places of worship. But these proved in many ways unsuitable, and Muslim architects developed new and distinctive styles of architecture, suited to the special needs of Muslim worship. Surviving masterpieces of this new, Islamic architecture include the famous mosques of Damascus in Syria and Cordoba in Spain.

In the Friday public prayer, the worshippers stand side by side in rows, facing the wall which shows the direction of Mecca. Unlike most other places of worship, the mosque is, therefore, usually planned in breadth with naves parallel to that wall. The worshippers are led by the imam, whom they must follow exactly. Traditionally, there is special merit in being in the front row, preferably to the right of the imam. In the earlier mosques, in the Arab lands, the place of worship was usually a wide chamber opening on a great open court. When Islam was brought to colder climates, however, an enclosed and sheltered space

The Umayyad Mosque of Damascus, Syria.
(Alistair Duncan ©Dorling Kindersley)

was needed. Ottoman and other Muslim architects found various solutions to this, notably the use of a large cupola resting on walls on a hexagonal plan. The arrangement in breadth and the absence of central supports left room for wide rows of worshippers, with a clear and unbroken view of the imam.

The interior of the mosque is simple and austere. There is no altar and no sanctuary, since there is no priest and no sacrament. Nor are there any seats or pews in the mosque. The worshippers may stand, bow, kneel, or prostrate themselves, but they do not sit in the House of God. There are, however, carpets. The act of worship includes prostrations, to the point where the worshipper's forehead touches the ground.

To participate in the ritual prayers, Muslims must be ritually pure. This is accomplished by means of ablutions, the manner and sequence of which are specifically regulated. To preserve the purity of the floor on which the worshipper prostrates himself, it is forbidden to enter the mosque wearing shoes or boots. These must be left at the entrance, and the worshipper—or, for that matter, visitor—must enter barefoot or with special slippers provided at the entrance. The need for purity precludes the participation or even the presence, during the prayers, of non-Muslims. Some forbid non-Muslims to enter the mosque in any circumstances. The more usual position is to admit them as visitors, but not during prayer.

This famous mosque in Istanbul, completed in 1616, is sometimes known by the name of its founder, Sultan Ahmet I. It is also known as the Blue Mosque because of its magnificent walls of Iznik tiles.

It was the first mosque outside Mecca to have six minarets. According to an early story, the Sultan told the architect he wanted a golden minaret, "altin" in Turkish. The architect misheard him and thought he said "alti," which in Turkish means six. The architect feared punishment for his mistake, but the Sultan was happy with the result.

A familiar feature of the mosque, in every part of the Muslim world, is the minaret, a tower usually attached to the mosque. It would seem that the minaret did not exist during the lifetime of the Prophet but first became a distinctive emblem of Islam in the period of the early Islamic conquests. It served a double purpose—as an emblem asserting Islamic presence and dominance and as a platform for calling the faithful to prayer. The call to prayer is performed by the mu'ezzin, a mosque functionary who summons the faithful to the five daily prayers and to public communal worship on Fridays. The distinctive call of the mu'ezzin is a characteristic feature of Muslim cities and communities. Thanks to modern technology, the call to prayer is now amplified and broadcast, sometimes prerecorded.

Minaret in Jerusalem. The mu'ezzin calls the faithful to prayer from the fenced walkway. When the call to prayer is from a recording, loud speakers are necessary.

The minaret exemplifies both the unity and variety of the Islamic world. Everywhere it serves the same religious and social purpose, soaring over the crowded alleys and markets, a signal and a warning to the believer. But at the same time, each region of the Islamic world developed its own style of minaret, sometimes recalling an earlier model—the step-towers of Babylon, the steeples of Syria, the lighthouses of Egypt. In time, all traces of a non-Islamic or nonreligious past were effaced; what remained was the slender beauty of the Muslim minaret, pointing heavenward in a gesture of devotion and submission.

Another characteristic of the mosque is the *minbar*, a pulpit or similar structure, from which sermons are preached every Friday and important announcements made when necessary. In classical times, in countries acquired peacefully, the preacher in the mosque carried a staff; in countries added to the Islamic world by conquest, he carried a sword. At times when and in places where the mosque was still the political as well as the religious center of the community, it was from the minbar that the ruler or his representative made important announcements—a change of sovereign or governor, the beginning or end of a war, and the like. It was an effective way of launching a rebellion. It is still often used for political statements.

The sermon preached in the mosque during the Friday prayer is known as the *Khutba* (see p. 201). In early times, this was often a political statement made by or on behalf of the sovereign or administrative head of the area. Later, it became a predominantly religious ceremony and was delivered by a preacher known as the *Khatib*. Being named as the ruler or governor in the Khutba is one of the recognized prerogatives of sovereignty in Islam; omission from the Khutba is a recognized declaration of rejection and revolt. In modern times, the Khutba has become a favorite medium of ideological, political, and similar declarations. The adoption of public address systems and then of the Internet has given it a new, wider, deeper impact.

Though Islam has no priesthood in the strict sense of that word, nevertheless there are, and have been since early times, members of the community with specialized knowledge who performed specialized functions and who evolved, in the course of time, into the functional though not the theological equivalent of a clergy.

A system of education and graduation evolved, though without anything resembling ordination. In Iran and other places where Persian cultural influence has been powerful, these men are known by the term *Mollah* or *Mullah*. The more usual term in Muslim countries for professional men of religion is *'ulama,* the plural of *'alim,* literally "one who knows," to denote religious knowledge.

ISLAMIC HUMOR

The story is told of a Turkish preacher who was invited to a mosque, to give three sermons at the public prayer on three consecutive Fridays. On the first Friday, he went up to the pulpit and asked the congregation: "Do you know what I am going to talk about?"

"No, preacher," they replied, "we don't."

"Well, if you don't know what I'm talking about, there's not much point in my talking to you," he said and went away.

The following week, when he went up to the pulpit to deliver his second sermon, he began with the same question: "Do you know what I am going to talk about?"

This time, they thought it wise to give the opposite answer: "Yes, preacher, we know."

"Well, in that case, since you know, there is no need for me to tell you." And he left the pulpit and went away.

One the third Friday, the preacher went up to the pulpit to deliver his third and last sermon and again began with the question: "Do you know what I am going to talk about?"

The community had been consulting all week about this, and they had come up with what they thought was the best answer: "Some of us know, and some of us don't know."

To this he answered: "Let those who know tell those who don't know." And he came down from the pulpit and was not seen again.

These professional men of religion are concerned with a number of things. Two of the most important and universal are prayer and law. The leader in prayer in the mosque was from early times known as the imam (see p. 197) who, in due course, also developed pastoral functions. The administration of religious law, which in Islam embraced every aspect of human and social life, is the special concern of two functionaries, the qadi and the mufti. The first is a judge in a court administering Shariʿa law; the second is a jurisconsult, a scholar specializing in the finer points of Islamic law and jurisprudence. There are many biographies of qadis and muftis from early medieval times onward and, from these, it is clear that any contact with the state authority was seen as demeaning. A standard theme in pious biography is that the hero is offered an appointment under the state and refuses it. The offer demonstrates his reputation—the refusal, his integrity and piety.

ISLAMIC HUMOR

The caliph chose a scholar whom he wanted to appoint as qadi. The scholar refused, saying that he did not have the necessary qualifications for this post.

The caliph replied: "You are lying, for you are surely one of the best scholars of our time."

The scholar replied: "You have proved my point, O Commander of the Faithful, by testifying that I am a liar."

Inevitably, in the course of time, the qadi and mufti were taken over by the state. The qadi, in order to make his judgments enforceable, had to have the state authority behind him, and in due course, he and his court of law became part of the state apparatus. For a long time, the mufti remained an independent religious scholar, giving not judgments but opinions, independent of state authority. But opinions evolved into rulings and, in the course of time, the mufti too was taken over by the state. In the Ottoman Empire, muftis were appointed by the government, each with a territorial jurisdiction and ranked in a hierarchy headed by the Chief Mufti of the capital. By this time, they had become the functional—though still not the theological—equivalents of bishops and their archbishop. In the late 19th century, yet a new title emerged among the Shiʿa of Iran—the title of Ayatollah (see p. 182).

In the Islamic Republic of Iran, the Ayatollahs have become the functional though not doctrinal equivalent of the College of Cardinals, and their leader, the Supreme Guide, might be described as a counterpart in some, though by no means all, respects of the Pope. Among Muslim minority communities in predominantly Christian countries, the mosque and its personnel have inevitably acquired some aspects of the church and churchmen in the West.

A common feature of modern mosques is the crescent, usually at the top of the minaret. In modern times, the crescent has come to be generally accepted, in Muslim lands and elsewhere, as the emblem of the Islamic religion, in the same way that the cross is the emblem of Christianity and the shield of David or six-pointed star is the emblem of Judaism. This is a modern development, and the use of these emblems in this way is an interesting example of projection and acceptance, from a dominant culture to others. In Christianity, the symbolism of the cross is clear and obvious. For a Christian, it represents the central event of human history and the central doctrine of his faith. Neither the shield of David nor the crescent has any such significance or evokes any such symbolism. Both have been used, by Jews and Muslims respectively, as decorative motifs, sometimes with religious overtones. But it is only recently, as part of the process of modernization—that is, the dissemination of the manners and customs of Christendom—that the crescent has come to be accepted as the emblem of Islam in the same way that the cross is the emblem of Christianity.

It was not so in the past. In early Islamic times, the only religious significance of the crescent was in relation to the calendar and, in particular, in determining the beginning and end of certain Muslim fasts and feasts. Muslims of most persuasions determine their religious calendar by observation, not by calculation and, therefore, such important events as the start of the pilgrimage (see *Hajj*, p. 193) and the beginning and end of the month of Ramadan (see Chapter 2, "The Pillars of the Faith") are determined by the sighting of the crescent or new moon. (Koran 2:183–189.) In medieval and early modern times, the crescent appears frequently as a decorative theme but, significantly, it has no standard form. It comes in various shapes, sometimes one, sometimes several, sometimes combined with a five-, six-, or even seven-pointed star. Its occasional use as a royal emblem probably dates back to pre-Islamic Iranian practice. This may also explain its use on buildings, coins, documents, and so on. The earliest dated textile decorated with crescents is a pair of light-blue silk trousers, made for the Ottoman sultan Suleyman the Magnificent (died 1566) and preserved in the Topkapi Palace Museum in Istanbul. It is, to say the least, highly unlikely that an Ottoman sultan would have used a religious emblem on his pants in this way.

Christians, however, following the normal human practice of seeing others in terms of themselves, assumed that the crescent was the emblem of Islam and in time even persuaded the Muslims to accept and use it as such. This happened in the early 19th century, when the reforming Ottoman sultans first created a European-style army, with European-style weapons and uniforms, and with other European innovations, notably a brass band and a flag. This flag, consisting of a crescent and a star on a red field, became and, with a few interruptions, remained the official flag of the Ottoman Empire and, after its demise, of the Turkish republic. It was later adopted in Tunisia and Egypt and, in the course of the 20th century, by many of the newly independent Muslim states. A red crescent on a white background was also recognized as equivalent by the International Committee of the Red Cross. It also appeared on the first Ottoman postage stamp, issued in January 1863. It has now also been officially designated by the United States government as the emblem to be used on headstones for Muslim veterans of the U.S. forces in national cemeteries. Of much greater antiquity is the sanctity attached in Muslim tradition to the color green, associated with the Prophet himself, and after him, with his descendants. Green is still sometimes used to symbolize Islam, but not in any formal or official way.

The mosque, from the earliest times, was a place not only of worship but also of study—indeed, in the Muslim perception, the two are intimately and inextricably linked. From early times, classes were held in the mosques, in which children—and sometimes adults—were taught the essentials of the faith and, more particularly, the obligations of the believer. These evolved into organized schools and colleges, and a new term—*madrasa*—was created to denote them. The literal meaning of the term is "a place of study." In earlier times, it was used to designate a college of higher studies, that is, above the primary and secondary levels, and was the equivalent—and in many ways, the predecessor and inspirer—of the European universities. In modern times, it has come to designate a sort of religious boarding school, usually associated with a mosque. At the present time, many of these are heavily subsidized by Saudi Arabia, and the services they offer—tuition, board, and lodging—are free. In many parts of the Muslim world, the madrasa is the only form of education available. Among the new, growing Muslim minorities in the Christian world, they perform an increasingly important function. It is very natural that Muslims living abroad should wish to give their children some grounding in their faith and culture. The madrasas—with a new and growing range of evening classes, weekend schools, holiday camps, and the like—meet this need.

Muslim communal worship is a disciplined act of submission to the One, immaterial God. It admits no drama and no mystery and, therefore, has no need for either music or poetry, still less for painting or statuary, which the Muslim tradition rejects as blasphemy verging on idolatry. The interior decoration of the mosque consists mainly of abstract and geometrical designs, often of tiles, with an extensive use of inscriptions on walls and ceilings.

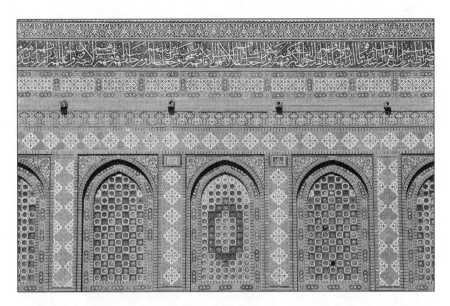

Tile work on the Dome of the Rock, Jerusalem. Among the Koranic quotations in the Dome is one that says, "There is no God but God alone, He has no companion....(9:33). "He is God, one, eternal; He does not beget nor is He begotten. (112:1-3).
(Corbis RF)

Inscriptions are in Arabic, regardless of the language of the country in which the mosque is situated. They include the names of God, the Prophet, the Muslim creed, verses or even whole chapters from the Koran, and, in Sunni mosques, the names of the early caliphs, known to the Sunni tradition as the "rightly guided" ones. Since the text of the Koran is, for Muslims, divine, to write it, read it, or look at it is, in a sense, an act of worship. In the course of time, Muslims in many lands evolved many ways of writing the Arabic script and developed an art of calligraphy of intricate and recondite beauty. These calligraphic texts are the equivalent of the hymns, fugues, and icons of other religions. They are a key to the understanding both of Islamic piety and of Muslim aesthetics.

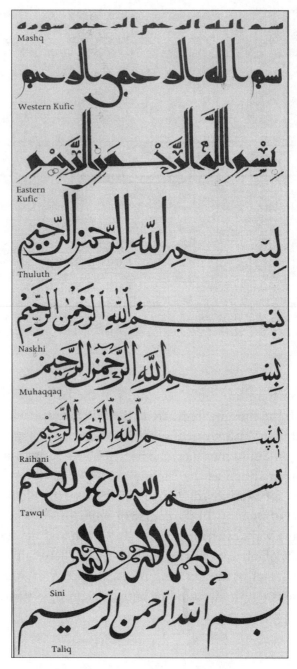

Ten calligraphic versions of the Arabic phrase
"In the name of Allah, the Merciful and the Compassionate."
(Scanned image used with permission from Brown Reference Group)

CHAPTER 5

Diversity and Tolerance

In traditional Islam, diversity, within certain limits, was seen as not only acceptable, but even beneficial. This diversity finds its most characteristic expression in the emergence, within Sunni Islam, of four different schools of doctrine and law, each with its own centers of learning, masters, and literature. These differ from each other on a number of points, but each respects the others as forming part of the community of orthodox Islam (see pp. 30-36).

The use of the term orthodoxy in a Muslim context raises another issue. Orthodoxy is a Christian, originally Platonic, term meaning "correct belief," as opposed to heterodoxy, literally "other belief," and, worse, "heresy." Heresy, a Greek word meaning "choice," soon took on a negative connotation and was specialized to mean "wrong choice." It was used from early times in Christian literature to designate doctrines that deviated from correct belief as formulated by constituted authority.

It is precisely on this point that Islam differs significantly from Christianity. Until comparatively modern times, there were in the world of Islam no constituted authorities empowered to define correct belief and thus, by implication, to define and condemn incorrect belief. For Muslims, as for Jews, what mattered was not so much correct belief as correct behavior, and it is to the definition and elaboration of these standards of correctness that much of the religious literature is devoted.

But of course, in a world as large as Islam, in a history as long as that of Islam, differences of doctrine and practice developed, and sometimes these went beyond what were generally regarded as the acceptable limits of diversity. The notion of "heresy" in the sense of incorrect belief remained alien to Islam. While the rich theological language of Islam contains names and descriptions of many heresies, it has no single word meaning heresy—or rather, it did not until the modern age, when a new word, *hartaqa*, was coined to express this notion. This word, now commonly used in Arabic, is obviously derived from the Western term heretic. In earlier times, beliefs and practices that did not conform to accepted norms and deviated from what one might call "mainstream Islam" were usually designated by terms meaning innovation, deviation, or excess. *Ghuluww*, "excess" or "exaggeration," is used for those groups, such as the Isma'ilis or the Druze, who carry their deviation beyond the generally acceptable limits of diversity. The term *bid'a*, literally "novelty" or "innovation," is used to condemn those who violate sacred precedents by introducing new ideas. The term is thus, in a sense, the opposite of Sunna, denoting the precept and practice of the Prophet. Some Muslims took the view that any such innovation must of necessity be false and evil; others recognized that new situations might arise, requiring new rulings, and made a distinction between good and bad bid'a. The general presumption, however, was that innovation as such was bad unless shown to be good. This perception was extended from religion to other matters and became a serious obstacle to development and progress.

From the record, it will be clear that in general, Islam, as a religion, community, and authority, has been remarkably tolerant of diversity within its own ranks. But there are limits and, at a certain point, the deviant Muslim ceases to be a Muslim and becomes a *kafir*, an unbeliever.

To be a kafir among kafirs is no problem, provided that his form of unbelief meets certain Muslim requirements for tolerance. But if one who has been or claims to be a Muslim is judged to be a kafir, this is a much more serious offense, and he is deemed to be an apostate. According to the prevailing interpretation of the holy law, this is a capital offense, and the offender must be put to death, whatever the circumstances. In this interpretation, even if he later repents and reverses his apostasy, he must still be executed. God may forgive him, but no human authority is empowered to do so. This penalty applies even in the case of a new convert to Islam, of however brief duration, who reverts to his previous faith. The death penalty normally included not only the convert but also anyone responsible for converting him. The term *takfir*, meaning "to denounce one who claims to be a Muslim but is in fact an infidel," has come into increasingly common use and is used to condemn those who diverge beyond what are seen as the permitted limits. A charge of takfir is in effect a charge of apostasy, a capital offense in most systems of Islamic law (see p. 219). In the traditional Muslim state and society, takfir normally meant a judgment or ruling by an Islamic court or dignitary, executed by the police or other public authority. In some, though by no means all, modern Muslim states, execution for a change of opinion is no longer acceptable. In practice, sadly, this has often meant that the classical procedure of trial and sentence has been replaced by incitement and murder. The same problems and similar solutions arise in a more acute form among Muslim communities living in non-Muslim countries and, therefore, not subject to Islamic law.

The most obvious form of apostasy is the abandonment of Islam and the adoption of another religion. The usually strict enforcement of this rule has been a major impediment to the work of the Christian missions. In some Muslim countries, such as Saudi Arabia, they are totally forbidden. In some others, such as Syria and Lebanon, their work has been in effect limited to converting Christians from one church to another.

In addition to an explicit renunciation of the faith, some actions, for example, certain forms of blasphemy, are considered tantamount to apostasy and incur the same penalties. It was on this basis that the

Ayatollah Khomeini accused the Anglo-Indian novelist Salman Rushdie of having insulted the Prophet and issued a fatwa sentencing him to death. A more insidious form of apostasy, from the traditional point of view, was the introduction of new and strange ideas and doctrines under the guise of Islam. Some of these, following new prophets, became in effect new religions. Such, for example, are the Ahmadiyya and the Baha'is. The first of these was founded in the 19ᵗʰ century by Mirza Ghulam Ahmad in the Punjab; the second in Iran, by Baha'allah (1817–1892). In 1868 he was banished from Iran and settled in Acre, which was then in the Ottoman Empire, now in Israel. It remains the world center of the Baha'i faith. Both of these groups were at times denounced and persecuted as apostates; both in time achieved a measure of sometimes precarious tolerance. Baha'ism is forbidden in the Islamic Republic of Iran.

From the traditionalist point of view, the danger presented by such movements is limited and has been contained. A much more menacing form of apostasy, according to that view, is the wave of new ideas coming from the West. And against these, new and more powerful responses have been developed.

Diversity within the community poses the most severe test of religious tolerance and, by this test, the record of Islam does not compare badly with that of other religions. True, there have been polemics and persecutions, insurrections and even wars but, until our own day, nothing remotely comparable with the inquisitions and persecutions, the insurrections and wars, that mar the history of Christendom until the rise of secularism. Even today, when intra-Islamic conflict has reached unprecedented levels of bitterness and ferocity, it has not yet reached that level, and there is still hope that this may be averted.

Another test of tolerance, less searching but no less important, concerns the attitude toward followers of other religions—of the believers toward those whom they regard as unbelievers.

On this point, there is a clear distinction between two types of religion, designated by their critics and opponents as relativist and triumphalist. Both are terms of abuse. The relativist view of religion is that just as men have invented different languages to talk to each other, so they have invented different religions to talk to God, and God understands them all—perhaps not equally well, but well enough. The classical formulation of this approach is contained in the Jewish Talmud, where it is said that the righteous of all peoples have a place in heaven. The righteous are defined as those who observe certain rules—monotheism and the basic social and ethical rules of human society. Triumphalists, in contrast, believe that they are the fortunate recipients of God's final message to mankind, which it is their duty not to keep selfishly to themselves, like the Jews, Hindus, and others, but to bring to the rest of humanity, removing whatever obstacles there may be in the way. The two obvious examples of this perception are Christianity and Islam.

Between two such religions, with a shared past, similar aspirations, and almost identical self-perceptions, living in adjoining areas, conflict was inevitable and gave rise to the long sequence of jihad and crusade, conquest and reconquest, starting with the advent of Islam in the 7th century of the Christian era.

In the Muslim perception, those who do not accept Muhammad as Prophet and the Koran as God's scripture are unbelievers. But not all unbelievers are the same, and there is a clear distinction between what one might call the predecessor religions and the rest. In the Muslim perception, Muhammad was the last in a long series of Prophets, and the Koran the final perfection of a series of books of revelation. Of these earlier groups of believers, the Koran names three: the Jews, the Christians, and the Sabians. Two have survived, each with their own revealed book: the Torah, that is, the five books of Moses, and the Gospels. But these earlier revelations had been disregarded and, worse, corrupted. They were, therefore, superseded and totally replaced by the final perfection of the Koran.

Nevertheless, these groups of earlier recipients of divine revelation were different from the polytheists and idolaters who comprised the rest of mankind and, therefore, qualified for a certain measure of tolerance in Muslim society and under the rule of the Muslim state. This tolerance is ordained and in some measure defined in the Koran, the traditions of the Prophet, and the rules of the holy law. The basic rules and limits of this tolerance are clearly set forth. Members of these three groups are to be allowed the free exercise of their religions in their own places of worship. They should be invited but not compelled to embrace Islam. If they persist in their unbelief, they may continue to practice their old religions, but subject to a poll-tax and some other disabilities, variously defined. These are set forth in a kind of pact or contract known as the *dhimma*, and those who participated in it were called *dhimmi*, the term normally used for the tolerated non-Muslim subjects of the Muslim state. The dhimma was only available to the permitted religions. For others, regarded as polytheists and idolaters, the options were conversion to Islam or death, which might be commuted to slavery and service. In fact, as Islam spread eastward first into Persia and then into India, it was found expedient to extend the scope of toleration to include other religions. For this purpose, the enigmatic Sabians were useful.

The enforcement, even the definition of the status of dhimmi, has varied enormously at different times and places in the fourteen centuries of Muslim history. In our own day, as with so many other aspects of Islamic history and culture, it has given rise to two contrasting myths: the one of a ferocious and unremitting persecution, the other of an interfaith utopia of complete equality and harmonious cooperation.

As is usual with such myths, both contain elements of truth; both are wildly, at times absurdly, distorted. As noted, practice varied greatly in different places and periods. But this much could be said with a reasonable certainty, that until the rise of secularism in Europe from the 17th century onward, the position of non-Muslims in the Muslim world was in general far better than the position of non-Christians or, still worse, deviant Christians in most Christian countries.

The clash between Christian Europe and the Muslim Ottoman Empire from the 15th to the 17th century has sometimes been compared to the clash between the West and the Soviet Union in more recent times. The comparison has some validity, but in making it, one should recall that in the earlier clash between Christendom and Islam, the movement of refugees, of those who in Lenin's famous phrase voted with their feet, was overwhelmingly from west to east and not, as in more recent times, from east to west.

The most obvious form of discrimination was the payment of the *jizya*, the poll-tax levied on non-Muslim subjects of a Muslim state. The jizya varied both in amount and in manner of collection. In some times and places, it was collected at a flat rate, and at other times, at different rates according to income. In the Ottoman Empire, the collection of jizya was entrusted to the various communities, who combined it with their own communal taxes on their own subjects and remitted an agreed amount to the state treasury. In principle, they were not allowed to build new places of worship, but only to maintain and where necessary to renovate old ones. In practice, this rule was usually disregarded, and many new churches and synagogues were built in lands under Muslim rule. One ban, however, was strictly enforced. In no circumstances were non-Muslims permitted to build places of worship that overtopped Muslim buildings. According to a classical dictum, "Islam overtops; it is not overtopped." Other disabilities included a ban on riding horses (donkeys were permitted) and bearing arms, and the imposition or prohibition of certain garments and the wearing of distinguishing signs or marks. These, like other rules, were sometimes rigorously enforced, sometimes intermittently, sometimes not at all.

By the standards of modern democracy, these forms of discrimination are, of course, unacceptable. But at the time, they represented a considerable improvement on what was available elsewhere and even included one element missing in the modern open society—that of communal autonomy. In the Ottoman Empire, until the 19th century reforms, dhimmi communities, Jews and Christians of various churches, formed their own communities, under their own heads and subject to their own laws, administered by their own courts, in such matters as marriage and divorce, inheritance, and much else. This autonomy included education, jurisdiction of their own courts in civil matters and, even in some criminal matters, of a religious nature. Thus, a Christian could be tried and punished by a Christian court for bigamy, or a Jew by a Rabbinic court on a charge of violating the Sabbath, though these were in no sense offenses against the generally accepted laws of the state and of the society.

The laws of the state were only enforced on the religious minorities where matters of public security were involved. Otherwise non-Muslims were exempt from rules that were strictly enforced against Muslims. Thus, for example, wine was, in accordance with their faith, forbidden to Muslims, but Jews and Christians were free to make, sell, and drink it without interference. There is an agonized correspondence in the Ottoman archives of the 16th century about an urgent problem of the time—how to prevent Muslim guests at Jewish and Christian weddings from drinking wine. The obvious and simple answer—a total ban—was apparently not considered. Curiously, the question of eating pork does not seem to have come up. Wine was obviously the greater temptation, and the wine tax a useful source of revenue.

The rising power of Christendom—first in the reconquest of some of the lost Christian lands, then in the extension of Christian power to Muslim lands—posed the problem of toleration in a new form—one in which the Muslim was the recipient, not the dispenser.

The juristic and theological discussion of this question began at an early date. At first, it was limited to those few Muslims who traveled or were taken to non-Muslim countries. The first group consisted of diplomats and merchants, the second of prisoners of war and slaves. The question acquired a new urgency with the advance of the Christian reconquest—in Spain and Portugal, in Sicily and, for a brief interval, in the Near East during the Crusades.

Two views crystallized among the jurists discussing this question. According to the first, Muslims must emigrate, since it is not possible to live a true Muslim life under infidel rule. Following the example set by the Prophet in his migration from pagan Mecca to Medina, they must go to a place where they can freely practice their religion, until such time as they can return as conquerors to their homes. According to a dissenting view, Muslims might remain in their homes under the rule of infidel conquerors, provided that they were free to practice their religion and fulfill their religious duties. As more and more Muslim countries came under Christian rule, notably in the British, French, and Russian empires, emigration ceased to be a practical possibility and adjustment became necessary. In the event, this proved not to be too difficult, since the imperial powers were for the most part cautiously conservative in their treatment of their new Muslim subjects and preferred not to interfere with existing practice. In some areas, as for example in the African colonies, the Islamization of society and the replacement of African custom by Islamic law proceeded apace under the Imperial yoke.

Muslim communities living as minorities in non-Muslim countries fall into two main groups. One of these, the more recent, is the new communities established by migration in Europe, the Americas and, to some extent, Australasia. The second group is the Muslim communities left behind in countries which were once part of the Muslim world but are no longer. The most important of these is India, where a community of many millions remains, from the time of Islamic conquest and domination. Smaller groups remain in southeastern Europe, in lands that once formed a part of the Ottoman Empire. These include, notably, the Muslim communities in Albania, Kossovo, and Bosnia. Other surviving Muslim communities are in the Russian Federation and in the central Asian regions of China, in countries that were at one time ruled by one or other of the great Muslim or Islamized empires in central Asia. To these we may add Israel, with a Muslim population comprising approximately one-fifth of the total.

What never seems to have occurred to any of the jurists in any place at any time was that Muslims would voluntarily migrate from Muslim lands to infidel lands and become residents, even citizens, of non-Muslim states. There are many reasons for this previously unthinkable migration, notably the great and growing discrepancy between the economic and social situations—standard of living, opportunity, public services—between the Islamic and the Western worlds. This has led to a massive migration from the Muslim lands of Asia and Africa into Europe and recently also to many countries in North, Central, and South America. By migration, demography and, to a significant degree, conversion, there are now large and growing Muslim communities in many of these countries. In the course of time, they pass from the status of immigrants to that of legal residents and, in due course, citizens by naturalization. In most though not all places, the second generation, born in the country, are citizens by birth.

How are they treated in their new homes, and how does this treatment compare with their expectations, with what they regard as their legitimate rights? The answers to these questions vary considerably according to differences both of reality and of perception. In material things, most would agree, they are better off than they were at home, in terms of standard of living and of social services. In terms of status, or in Western language, of rights, they are getting both more and less than what they expect and see as an entitlement. In terms of economic opportunity and of political and social self-expression, they enjoy opportunity and access vastly better than in almost any Muslim country. On the other hand, they are denied the autonomous communal status that was granted as a matter of course to non-Muslim minorities in most Muslim countries in an increasingly remote past.

Despite the efforts of some European governments to be accommodating in this matter, for example by approving welfare payments to plural wives, these problems remain unresolved.

CHAPTER 6

Sunni, Shi'a, and Others

O f the differences that arose among Muslims, by far the most important, from early times to the present day, have been between the Sunnis and the Shi'a, and most of the Muslim world is divided between these two groups. Some have tried to explain this division by likening it to the split between Catholics and Protestants in Christendom. This is a false analogy and can easily be discredited by asking a simple question: "Which are the Protestants and which are the Catholics?" There can be no serious answer to this question, because the comparison itself is meaningless and misleading. The Christian difference between Protestants and Catholics—and earlier between the church of Rome and the Eastern (Orthodox) churches—arose basically over ecclesiastical authority. In Islam, there is not—or to be precise, there was not until modern times—anything that could really be called ecclesiastical authority, since there was nothing that could be called a church in the institutional sense of that term (see Chapter 4, "The Mosque").

The difference between Sunni and Shi'a goes back to the beginnings of Islam and was in its origins purely political—a dispute over the succession to the Prophet Muhammad as the head of the Muslim state and community which he had founded. When the Prophet died, the leaders of that community chose first one, then others of his senior followers to succeed him in what came to be known as the caliphate. At the time, there were some who believed that the succession belonged by right to the Prophet's family. The Prophet left no son, but he left a daughter, Fatima, who married his cousin Ali and was the ancestress of all the Prophet's descendants. The primary meaning of the Arabic word *Shi'a*

is "party" or "faction," and the supporters of Ali's claims to the caliphate came to be known as the Shi'a, that is, party, of Ali. In 656 CE,
after the murder of the third caliph Uthman by a group of Arab Muslim
mutineers, Ali succeeded him in the caliphate. But the circumstances
of his succession split the Islamic community and led to a civil war, in
the course of which Ali himself was murdered and replaced by another
Muslim leader.

The followers of Ali's sons, Hasan and Husayn, tried to overthrow
the ruling caliphs, whom they and their followers regarded as usurpers. Their rising was ruthlessly suppressed, and the martyrdom of
Husayn at Karbala in Iraq, some 60 miles southwest of Baghdad, on 10
Muharram 61 of the Muslim ura corresponding to 10 October 680 CE
marks an important date in the Shiite calendar.

Though their origins were, thus, primarily political and in a sense
personal, other differences developed between Sunni, or mainstream
Islam, and the Shi'a, who soon subdivided into a variety of factions,
originally supporting different claimants to the succession to Ali. In
most of the Muslim world, the Sunnis have been the dominant element,
the Shi'a the opposition. The differences arising from these contrasting
experiences have left their mark on Sunni and Shi'a beliefs, customs,
and in a few respects, even laws. The Shi'a, for example, allow *mut'a* (see
p. 114), a contract of marriage for a specified period, automatically dissolved at the end of that period; the Sunnis do not. The Shi'a also have a
doctrine of *taqiyya* (see pp. 219-220), which one might translate as dissimulation. Not surprisingly for a sometimes persecuted minority, they
accepted the principle that, in certain situations, it is permitted to dis-
simulate—that is, to conceal or even misstate one's beliefs. Originally a
mainly Shi'ite notion, taqiyya has enjoyed somewhat wider acceptance
and practice in modern times.

In the course of time, the Shi'a became the main opposition within
the Islamic state and society, supporting a series of claimants to the
caliphate, known to their followers as the Imams. All of these claimed
to be the descendants of Ali and Fatima and, thus, of the Prophet,
through different lines of descent.

Among the Shi'a as among the Sunnis, internal differences of both doctrine and practice arose, but no doubt because the Shi'a were usually in opposition and therefore under constraint, they proved less tolerant than the Sunnis of diversity. These splits usually arose over the succession to the Imamate, but sometimes developed into more important differences of both doctrine and practice.

The most important difference was between the so-called Twelver Shi'a and the Isma'ilis. The first major dispute began in 765 CE on the death of the sixth Imam in the line of succession of Ali and Fatima when the Shi'a split between two claimants. One group, the more conservative of the two, later came to be known as the Twelvers. The other group followed a rival claimant, Isma'il, and are still known as the Isma'ilis. For most of the Shi'a, there was a succession of twelve generations of Imams after Ali. The twelfth Imam disappeared circa 874 CE, leaving no successor. Among the Shi'a, he is known as "the hidden Imam," a Messianic figure who will return in God's good time. In some circles in the Islamic Republic in Iran, it is being strongly suggested that the hidden Imam has already returned and will soon emerge from hiding and inaugurate the sequence of events leading to the final establishment of the kingdom of heaven on earth.

In medieval times, Isma'ilism was a movement of considerable importance and even gave rise to one of the major dynasties of the medieval Islamic world, the Fatimid Caliphate, which ruled first North Africa, and then Egypt and its dependencies, between the 10th and 12th centuries and, for a while, offered a serious challenge to the Sunni caliphs of Baghdad for the headship of the Muslim world. Their regime was finally overthrown by the great Muslim hero Saladin, who reincorporated their domains into the world of Sunni Islam.

In the late Fatimid period, the Isma'ilis split into two groups, again following rival candidates for the succession. The split began in 1094 CE on the death of the Fatimid caliph al-Mustansir. Some of the Isma'ilis accepted his successor in the caliphate as the rightful Imam; others followed his brother Nizar. Both groups survive to the present day and are usually known by the names of Bohra or Bohora and Nizari. Their main centers are in the Indian subcontinent and Yemen, with smaller groups in central Asia and Syria and, by more recent migration, in parts of Africa and America. An offshoot of the Nizari Isma'ili movement was the famous order of Assassins (see pp. 181-182). The largest group of the Isma'ilis today are the Nizaris, whose Imam is known as the Aga Khan (see p. 180).

Two other groups, related to the extremist wing of the Shi'a, should be mentioned. The first are the Alawis or Alawites, chiefly represented in Turkey and in Syria, where they are also known as Nusayris. The Alawis are regarded as deviants alike by the Twelver Shi'a, the Isma'ilis, and, of course, most of all, by the Sunnis. They nevertheless form an important minority in both countries. In Syria, the reigning dynasty of presidents of the Asad family, now in its second generation, are Alawis, and the main basis of their power is in the Alawi territories in the northwest part of the country. In Turkey, where they are known as Alevi, they benefitted significantly from the secularist policies of the republic but were and are otherwise regarded with suspicion by the Sunni establishment.

The second are the Druze, a group of followers of the Fatimid Caliph al-Hakim (reigned 996–1021 CE), to whom they accord a quasi-divine status. They form a more or less secret religious sect, located mainly in Lebanon, Syria, Israel, and Jordan. No one is permitted either to leave or to join their community. They have at times played an important role in local history, notably in Lebanon. In the state of Israel, since its foundation in 1948, the Druze minority, unlike the other Arab communities, are included, at their own request, in the draft, from which other non-Jews are exempt. As their leaders put it at the time, they wanted to enjoy the full rights of citizenship in the new state and felt that they could not achieve this without accepting the burdens as well as the rights.

At the beginning of the 16th century, a new development occurred in Iran, which brought a radical change in the relationship between Sunni and Shi'a all over the Middle East. The immediate cause of this change was the seizure of power by a new dynasty, the Safavids, who were themselves followers of the Twelver Shi'a faith. They accomplished two major changes. One was the reunification of the historic realm of Iran, which for centuries had been conquered and ruled by a succession of invaders—Arabs, Turks, and Mongols—and divided into different provinces and principalities. The Safavids reconstituted the ancient empire and resumed the ancient title of Shah used by the emperors of the pre-Islamic era.

The second major change was that they proclaimed Twelver Shiism to be the state religion of the Iranian realm. This gave an ideological base to the newly recovered Iranian unity and identity and, at the same time, marked them off from their Sunni neighbors in the Ottoman lands to the west, Muslim India to the east, and Muslim central Asia to the North. A long conflict ensued between the Ottoman sultans and the shahs of Iran, a resumption, in a sense, of the conflict in antiquity between the Greco-Roman world and the Persians.

The rivalry took several forms: a struggle for control of the border province of Iraq, long contested between the two, and a larger competition for supremacy in the Middle East and the broader world of Islam. There were, of course, many Sunnis in Iran and many Shi'a in the Ottoman Empire, and this gave a new sharpness and, at times, a new urgency to the differences between their two versions of the Islamic faith. During the long Ottoman-Iranian rivalry, we find occasional persecutions, even inquisitions, but these were more concerned with sedition and treason than with incorrect belief and worship. And at their worst, they never reached the level of the bitter and bloody wars of religion that followed the Reformation in Europe.

The difference between Sunni and Shi'a originally arose over the headship of the Muslim community. In the course of time, some differences of law and doctrine evolved, but these are of comparatively minor importance. The really significant differences between the two arose from their different experience—the one of dominance, the other of subordination and all the social and psychological consequences of this difference.

At the present day, the Sunnis are certainly the great majority in the Muslim world as a whole. Only Iran and Iraq have Shi'a majorities; only Iran has for centuries been ruled by Shi'ite governments which enforced Shi'ite law. In Iraq, the Sunni minority has ruled the Shi'a majority since the beginning of Islamic rule, except for a brief interval in the 16th century, when Iraq was incorporated in the domains of the Shi'ite shahs of Persia. Iraq was, for a while, contested between the Sunni Ottoman sultans and the Shi'ite Persian shahs, but the former prevailed. Even after the fall of the Ottoman Empire, through the time of the British mandate, the Iraqi Hashimite monarchy, and the various dictators who followed its downfall, the Sunni minority has dominated the Shi'a majority. Recent events in Iraq have brought significant changes, notably the formation of a Shi'a-led government would seem to indicate that the long Sunni ascendancy may be coming to an end.

There are Shi'a minorities in Syria and Lebanon, Saudi Arabia, and the Gulf states, India and Pakistan, and some other places. Shi'ism seems to be almost completely absent from the Islamic countries of Africa, except for fairly recent immigrants from south Asia.

Another group that differed from the Sunni mainstream was the Kharijites. Like the Shi'a, they challenged the Sunnis on the question of the caliphate, but from the opposite direction. For them, any form of hereditary succession was unacceptable. The caliph should be chosen for his religious and moral qualities. He should be under continuous scrutiny for his behavior and could be deposed if at any time he was found not to meet the required standards. They too, therefore rejected the successive caliphates of Medina, Damascus, and Baghdad. In the early centuries of Islam, the Kharijites sometimes played an important role and presented a serious problem for various Islamic governments. At the present, only one branch of the Kharijite movement survives and is of some significance: the Ibadite movement, principally found in Oman, where it is the predominant form of Islam. Ibadis are also found in East and North Africa. Unlike some other Islamic groups, the Ibadis do not regard a Muslim who does not share their views as an infidel or a renegade, and they thus reject religiously inspired murder. They also allow intermarriage with non-Ibadi Muslims. In general, their doctrines and attitudes are similar to those of the Sunnis.

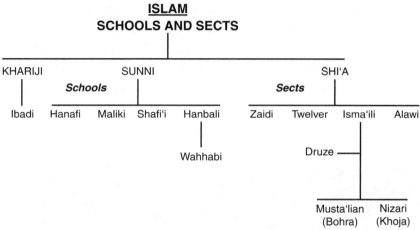

The schools and sects of Islam.

A movement of major importance among both Sunni and Shi'a Muslims was the movement known as Sufism. The term Sufi is commonly used to denote Muslim mystics. According to some, it is a loanword from the Greek *Sophia,* meaning "wisdom"; the more usual and more probable explanation derives it from *suf,* the name of rough woolen clothing worn by mystics and ascetics.

Sufism has had a profound and far-reaching impact throughout Islamic history. Mystical and ascetic movements of various kinds appeared at an early date in Islamic history and spread to almost all parts of the Islamic world. Sufis played a considerable role in the development of Islamic religion and, more broadly, Islamic civilization. They also aroused strong and, even at times, violent opposition.

The Sufi difference may be described under three headings:

1. **The mystical**—Sufi belief in the possibility and, therefore, desirability of achieving mystical union with God.
2. **The aesthetic**—Unlike what one might call mainstream Muslims, Sufis make considerable use of the arts in their

worship—notably poetry, music, and even the dance. In Middle Eastern antiquity, the dance was often an important part of public worship. Since David danced before the Ark of the Lord (1 Chronicles 15:29), mainstream Judaism, Christianity, and Islam alike have rejected the dance as a form of worship, though various sectarian groups have cultivated and practiced it. Some of the Sufi orders gave it a central role, notably those who came to be known as the dancing or whirling dervishes. Sufism has given rise to a rich tradition of mystical poetry in Arabic and still more in Persian and Turkish.

Whirling dervishes in Istanbul, Turkey.

3. **The ethical**—An example of the Sufi approach that was attractive to some and repellant to other Muslims may be found in the writings of Sheikh Sharaf al-Din Maneri (died 1381). According to him, a man's obligations to his fellow men are far more important than his obligations to God. If he fails in his obligations to God, God suffers no harm, and there is, therefore, no obstacle on the path to penitence and forgiveness. But offenses against one's

fellow men require that the offender make good the damage that he has done and obtain the forgiveness and even the intercession of the victim. Another Sufi teacher is cited as saying that rather than go on the pilgrimage, it is better to save the money that it would have cost and use it to help the poor.

Sufis are normally organized in brotherhoods or orders, known as *tariqa*, each with its own rules and rituals. The term *dervish*, probably of Persian origin, but of disputed etymology, is usually used to describe the members of these orders.

The Sufis have often been criticized and even rejected by Sunni theologians and are totally condemned by the Wahhabis. Not surprisingly, those who see religion primarily in terms of mystical union with God and helping their fellow men are often accused of negligence or worse in the fulfillment of religious duties, that is, such basic commandments of the faith as prayer, fasting, and pilgrimage. There are many popular anecdotes in Muslim countries that play on this theme.

ISLAMIC HUMOR

The dervishes were often accused of being negligent in such mundane religious duties as prayer and fasting. A popular anecdote tells of a dervish who was caught eating during the fast of Ramadan, at a time when divine commandments were still enforced by human authority. He was promptly arrested and thrown into jail. Looking out between the bars of his prison window, he saw a man in the street outside, eating a kabab. The dervish called out to him:

"Hey you, you are eating a kabab."

"Yes," said the man, "I am eating a kabab—so what?"

The dervish said: "Don't you know it's Ramadan? If they see you, they'll arrest you and throw you into jail where I am."

"No, they won't," said the man with the kabab, "I am a Christian."

"You mean," said the dervish, "that because you are a Christian, you are allowed to eat kabab in the street in broad daylight during Ramadan?"

"Yes," said the man, "these rules only apply to Muslims, not to us."

The dervish sighed and said to the man: "You should give thanks to Allah every day that you are not of the true faith."

CHAPTER 7

Some History

B etween 1980 and 1988, a bitter and deadly war was fought between two Muslim countries in the Middle East: Iraq and Iran. The rulers of both countries made extensive use of the mass media to direct their propaganda both at their own people and at those of the enemy—to sustain the one and subvert the other. In this, as in so much else, they were following the examples offered to them by the European powers, notably in the Second World War and, in its aftermath, the Cold War.

But in one respect, the war propaganda, on both sides, was strikingly different from that of the European and American powers, and that was in the use of history. The propaganda spread by both the Iraqis and Iranians was full of allusions to past events. Remarkably, these allusions were not only to a recent but also, more intensively, to a distant past—to the seminal events of the 1st century of Islam, corresponding to the 7th and early 8th centuries of the Common Era. Still more remarkably, these allusions were not detailed narratives or stories of past events, but simple mentions of a name, place, date, or event, used in the sure knowledge that the allusion would be picked up and understood by their target audiences, even including the substantial part that was illiterate.

Both sides, in their propaganda, made frequent allusion to a great battle fought in or about 637 CE at a place called Qadisiyya, in Iraq, then part of the Persian Empire, between an Arab Muslim army from Arabia and the army of the Persian Emperor. The battle ended with a decisive victory for the Muslim Arabs, which led to the collapse of the Persian Empire and the incorporation of all its lands and peoples in the realm of Islam. Interestingly, both sides in the 1980s claimed this battle as a glorious victory for them over their enemies, and both were, in a sense, right. For Saddam Hussein and his nationalist target audience, it was a victory of Arabs over Persians. For the Islamic theocrats of Tehran, it was a victory of true believers over unbelievers, which brought the true faith to the previously heathen peoples of Iran. For both sides, it was an example to be followed, a triumph to be repeated.

This acute awareness of the past, even a distant past, is a characteristic feature of Islamic society and is in marked contrast with the growing disregard by Westerners of their own past. The common American phrase, "That's history," means it's over, finished, and of no present relevance or concern. Europe hasn't quite reached that point but seems to be moving in that direction.

The Muslim view is very different. For believing Muslims, Muhammad was the last of a sequence of prophets; the Koran was the final revelation, superseding all its predecessors. The course of events since then marks the fulfillment of God's purpose for humanity, and the historical record enables us to see and understand the nature of that purpose and the manner of its fulfillment.

For Muslims, naturally, history primarily means the history of Islam and of the Muslim community. Events outside the lands of Islam were, therefore, for traditional historians, of no importance; events prior to the advent of Islam, even in their homelands, were important only insofar as they shed light on the processes which led to that advent. This meant that, with rare exceptions, pre-Islamic history was known only from the allusions to that history contained in the Koran and the Muslim tradition—that is to say, a much abbreviated and sometime divergent version of the Biblical narratives. Astonishingly, the rich, diverse, and well-documented history of the great civilizations of the Middle East in antiquity was, until modern times, completely forgotten—their monuments neglected or destroyed, their writings buried and disregarded, their very languages and scripts unknown. The discovery of these ancient monuments, the decipherment of their scripts and languages, and the resulting recovery of whole new chapters of a forgotten yet glorious past were at first and for a long time entirely the work of Western, that is to say, European and later also American archaeologists, philologists, and historians.

FATE OR FREE WILL

Muslims, like others, have argued over the question: Is everything pre-determined by fate, that is, by God, or does humanity have a free choice? At first sight, it would appear that the Muslim verdict is clear, expressed notably in the Koranic verse: "Nothing shall befall us save what God has written down for us" (9:51). This is a favorite text of calligraphers and others, and elegantly written and framed versions of it may frequently be found in bazaars and other public places. Some Muslim authorities have considered this a clear statement of predestination and find confirmation of this interpretation elsewhere in the Koran and other texts.

There is, however, some variety in the way this doctrine is interpreted, and the most usual opinion has been to allow, within the framework of God's decrees, a certain amount of freedom of choice. An image used in a medieval Muslim tract explains this in terms of two popular games, both of Middle Eastern origin. Life is not a game of chess, based on complete free will. It is a game of backgammon, where destiny, in the form of the throw of the dice, limits our options, but leaves us free to choose between them, and to win or lose the game.

The work of these scholars, sometimes known as Orientalists, first became known through translations from European languages in the late 19th century and only gradually became part of the intellectual and cultural self-awareness of these countries. Until then, the name Pharaoh, in the land of the Pharaohs, was known only from the Koran and remained the prototype of the arbitrary pagan tyrant. A striking example is the following: In 1982, when a small group of Egyptian Muslim terrorists murdered President Sadat of Egypt, the leader of the group proudly proclaimed, "I have killed Pharaoh!" It was widely assumed at the time that Sadat was killed because he made peace with Israel. This was certainly disapproved by many, notably by the extreme Islamists, but if that was the prime charge against Sadat, calling him Pharaoh was, to say the least, an odd choice. Pharaoh, in the Koran as in the Bible, is the evil infidel who disregarded God's message, brought to him by God's prophet, in this case Moses, and oppressed God's people, in this case the children of Israel. The use of this image caused some soul-searching in Egypt at the time.

The leader of the assassins did not kill Sadat because he made peace with Israel, which he saw as a consequence rather than a cause of his evil; he killed him as an oppressor of God's people—the role of Pharaoh in the story of the Exodus, in the Koran as in the Bible. For Sadat's Islamist critics, his major offense was turning to the infidel West and trying to westernize Egypt, that is, to destroy its Islamic foundations. Some writers at the time went so far as to say that the struggle against Israel was of secondary importance and should be set aside until the main purpose, Islamic victory at home, was achieved. Then such lesser problems could be dealt with quickly and easily.

Like the Pharoanic Egyptians, so too the other great civilizations of the ancient Middle East— the Assyrians and Babylonians, the Hittites, the Medes, and the Persians—were all forgotten and remained unknown until they were recovered and restored to their descendants and successors by modern scholarship.

More recently, ancient history has become rather more important in public awareness and, therefore, in public discourse—more so with secular and nationalist regimes, less so with religious and Islamic regimes. The late Saddam Hussein included among his heroes both Saladin, who defeated the Crusaders, and Nebuchadnezzar, who disposed of the Jewish state in his day. The late Shah of Iran claimed and celebrated Cyrus as the founder of the Iranian monarchy. The Turks even developed an interest in the Hittites, the ancient inhabitants of Anatolia, who had the advantage of being neither Greek nor Christian. The rulers of the Islamic Republic of Iran cite only the Islamic period.

Since the advent of Islam, history has been important for Muslims, and Islamic historiography is extraordinarily rich and varied. It has been calculated that up to the end of the Middle Ages, historical writing in Arabic is more extensive than the entire output of the Western world, in Latin, Greek, and all the European vernaculars combined. For some time, Arabic was the only language used by Muslims for writing history. Later, new languages and literatures developed—Islamic versions first of Persian, then of Turkish, and then of other languages in Asia and Africa. Quite apart from explicitly historical literature, an awareness of history pervades most other forms of literature, notably religion, philosophy, and poetry, and writers feel free to make historical allusions in the sure knowledge that, as with the war propagandists of the 1980s, they will be picked up and understood.

In the Western world, from an early date, history is defined by nation or by country; indeed, for some, though not all, the two words are synonymous. In the Islamic world, identity and, therefore, loyalty were primarily defined by religion. History meant the history of the Islamic state and community; its content, for the purposes of historiography, was defined by the different dynasties of caliphs and sultans who headed the Islamic state and commanded its armies in the unending war against the unbelievers, that is, those countries and peoples that had not yet accepted the divine message and the authority that brought it to them. At a time when most Western historical writing was still dynastic and local, Muslim historians had a much broader, one might even say global, perception.

The ongoing struggle to bring the faith to the unbelievers was fought on three continents—in Asia, in Africa, and in Europe—and in all three of them, the advancing Muslims achieved considerable successes.

In the Muslim perception, the early centuries of Islam were a period of triumph and glory, when the Islamic armies advanced far into Asia and Africa, bringing the faith to many millions of benighted heathens. Moving eastward, they conquered the entire realm of the former emperors of Iran, and, advancing beyond its eastern frontiers, invaded Central Asia and India. Later, Muslim dynasties, from Iran and Central Asia, continued the conquest of India, which remained part of the realm of Islam until Muslim was replaced by British imperial rule.

More important than any of these, in the early stages of Islamic history, was the battle against the rival world faith, Christendom. Most the religions of the world are in some sense ethnic or local, or at most regional. Christians and Muslims resemble each other in their triumphalist and universalist perceptions.

Between two such religious communities, historically akin, geographically adjacent, with the same sense of global and cosmic mission, conflict was inevitable, and it continued for many centuries, in a long sequence of conquest and reconquest, jihad and crusade, and imperial rule both ways. In this struggle, the early Muslims were able to win significant victories, gaining Syria, Palestine, Egypt, and North Africa, at that time part of the Christian Roman Empire, and adding them to the realm of the caliphs. From Africa, they advanced still further into Europe, conquering Spain, Portugal, and southern Italy, and for a while seriously threatening even France.

That threat was met and held. A wave of Christian reconquest achieved the recovery of Spain, Portugal, and southern Italy, but was unable to recover North Africa nor—from a Christian point of view, most painful of all—the Holy Land of Christendom. Muslims were more fortunate in that their Holy Land, the Hijaz, with the holy cities of Mecca and Medina, remained at all times under Muslim rule, even in the worst periods of Muslim defeat and withdrawal. The Caliph Umar, the second ruler of the Islamic state and community after the death of the Prophet, decreed that no non-Muslims might dwell in or even visit the Holy Land of Islam. The indigenous Christian and Jewish communities were, therefore, transported elsewhere and resettled in Iraq and Palestine. The ban on non-Muslim presence or even entry remains in force today. The Christian holy places in the Holy Land have been under non-Christian rule from the Arab Islamic conquest in the 7th century to the present day, with two brief exceptions: the short-lived crusader kingdom in the Middle Ages and the British mandate for Palestine in the 20th century.

The loss of the relatively unimportant far West in the late Middle Ages was, from a Muslim point of view, more than compensated by the advance of Islam in the eastern Mediterranean: the conquest in the 11ᵗʰ century of the previously Christian land of Anatolia, the invasion of southeastern Europe, the capture of the Christian city of Constantinople in 1453, and the advance of the Ottoman Turks into Europe to rule the Balkan Peninsula and half of Hungary and threaten the very heart of Europe. As late as the 17ᵗʰ century, Muslim armies from Turkey were still invading central Europe; Muslim corsairs from North Africa were still raiding the coasts of western Europe, as far away as the British Isles, and even Madeira and Iceland.

The decisive and this time uncompensated change came with the defeat in 1683 of the final Turkish attempt to capture Vienna, and the beginning of the long retreat of the Muslim armies from most of the lands that they had conquered. Now Europe, or Christendom as it would have been called at the time, was on the counterattack and was soon proceeding from reconquest, the recovery of their own lost lands, to conquest, the invasion and domination of what were by now seen as the Islamic heartlands. From the north, two great Christian powers, Austria and Russia, advanced toward the Caspian, the Black Sea, and the Mediterranean; even more alarmingly, from the south, west Europeans, Portuguese, Dutch, French, and English, sailed around the Cape of Good Hope and attacked the Islamic lands of South and Southeast Asia on the other side. This created a new situation, in which Muslims saw their world threatened not just with the loss of this or that remote province, but by an attack on the very centers of their faith and power.

Their awareness of this change and of this new menace was much heightened by the fact of the annual pilgrimage, which every year brings great numbers of Muslims from all over the Muslim world, as far away as Morocco and Indonesia, central Asia and central Africa, to share the same rites at the same time in the same place. This gave rise to a kind of shared awareness of events, all over the Muslim world, that was without precedent in the Western world until the invention and use of the modern media.

By the end of the 18th century, Muslims all over the lands of Islam were becoming painfully and bitterly aware that they were endangered—worse, that they seemed to be losing the millennial struggle against the long familiar and previously despised Western adversary.

In the course of the 18th and 19th centuries, the dominance of the Christian European powers was extended and strengthened in most of the Muslim world. The Russians, expanding southward and eastward, incorporated the Muslim lands of the Caucasus and of much of north and central Asia into the empire of the Tsars. West European maritime powers were able to dominate much of south and southeast Asia. By the beginning of the 20th century, almost all the Muslim world was either ruled directly or controlled indirectly by the European empires. Only three countries retained their independence and some semblance of importance: Afghanistan, Persia and, on the frontier of Christendom, the Ottoman Empire. By 1918, Persia was marginalized and unimportant. The Ottoman Empire, the last of the great Sunni empires, was defeated and suffered a worse fate than either of its allies, Germany and Austria. Its capital was occupied, its ruler deposed, its territories partitioned between the victorious Allies. In Turkey proper, a secularist nationalist movement was able to restore and retain the independence of the Turkish heartland, but the rest of the Middle East was lost and, even at home, in the aftermath of war, the caliphate was abolished and the last caliph sent into exile. For Muslims, this was the lowest moment in their long and previously glorious history.

A question was now debated with increasing agony. How was one to hold and defeat the ancient enemy? How was one to recover the by now almost legendary greatness of the Islamic past? Understandably, the issue was intensely and painfully discussed all over the Muslim world.

The proposed solutions fell broadly into two categories. The first was that of what one might call the Westernizers—those who felt that the only way to hold and defeat the West was to learn from the West and defeat the invader by using his own weapons against him and become part of the modern world. This method was widely adopted by a number of Islamic rulers and leaders but had only limited success in achieving that aim. The one outstanding example was the triumphant emergence of the Turkish Republic in 1923 from the ashes of the defeated and destroyed Ottoman Empire. The other approach was that of those Muslims who saw Westernization not as the remedy but as the source of the disease. By abandoning the pure heritage of their ancestors and adopting the pernicious and destructive ways of the infidel, Westernizers had brought defeat and humiliation to Muslims everywhere. The remedy—for them, clear and unequivocal—was a return to what they saw and presented as authentic Islam. This movement first appeared in Arabia in the late 18th century. Since then, it has developed along several different lines and spread to much of the Islamic world.

ISLAMIC HUMOR

A group of courtiers and others were chatting one day at the court of the Caliph al-Mansur (reigned 754-776 CE), and the conversation turned to an old and much discussed subject—the nature of happiness. Various views, both religious and philosophical, were put forward, and eventually the group turned to the Caliph and asked him: "O Commander of the Faithful, tell us, who is a happy man?"

And the Caliph replied: "I don't know him and he doesn't know me."

CHAPTER 8

Government and Opposition

The religion of Islam, in contrast to both Judaism and Christianity, was involved in the conduct of government and the enactment and enforcement of law from the very beginning. Moses led his people out of slavery and through the wilderness but did not enter the Promised Land. He was a leader but never a ruler. Jesus was crucified, and his followers were a powerless, sometimes persecuted sect until, with the conversion of the Emperor Constantine circa 312 CE, they captured the Roman State and—some would add—were captured by it. Muhammad, in contrast, overcame his enemies and achieved power during his lifetime. According to the traditional narrative, he began his mission in Mecca, where he was born, and achieved some success in his preaching against the prevailing paganism. But the ruling pagan oligarchy reacted strongly and, the Prophet, with a group of his companions, moved to another town in the Hijaz, until then known as Yathrib, and from the time of the Prophet onward, as al-Madina, the city, usually transcribed Medina. In his new home, Muhammad was welcomed not just as a prophet and teacher but also as a ruler, and it was there that he created the first Islamic state, with himself as its sovereign head.

In Medina, the Prophet did what heads of state normally do: He promulgated and enforced laws, he collected taxes and, when necessary, he made war and then peace and, in general, conducted the political, fiscal, military, and judicial affairs of his community. Both phases of his career, of opposition and of government, are reflected in the Koran and in the prophetic traditions and biography.

When the Prophet Muhammad died in the year 632 CE, his followers confronted a difficult problem, succession in the headship of the religious community and political order which he had created. In his spiritual function, there could be no successor—according to Muslim belief, Muhammad was the last of the prophets, and the Koran was the last of God's revelations to mankind. But in addition to a religion in the narrower sense, he had headed a community and a state, and in both, a successor was urgently needed.

The dynastic principle was well known in Arabia as in the rest of the ancient world. Muhammad left no son, but his daughter was married to his kinsman Ali, and there were some who thought that Ali, the nearest male relative of the Prophet and the father of his grandchildren, was the most appropriate choice. They were not successful, and the Muslims looked elsewhere and chose as their leader Abu Bakr, known as al-Siddiq, the upright or truthful. One of the earliest converts to Islam, he was only three years younger than the Prophet and was one of the senior and most respected members of the community. His nomination seems to have been generally accepted among Muslims at the time.

But to what was he nominated? The Arabic language at the time offered a choice of titles with a connotation of chieftaincy or kingship. Abu Bakr and the Muslims chose none of these. Instead, he was given a new title—*khalifa*, a word which, by a portentous ambiguity, combines the meanings of deputy and successor.

But of whom? According to the Sunni Muslim historical tradition, Abu Bakr presented himself and was accepted as "Khalifa of the Prophet of God." According to an early historical narrative, when Abu Bakr died and was succeeded by Umar, the second caliph, a man hailed the new head as "Khalifa of God." Umar refused to make any such blasphemous claim, pointing out that he was the Khalifa not of God but of his predecessor: Khalifa of the Khalifa of the Prophet of God. Since this designation would obviously get longer and longer, he suggested a new and simpler form of titulature. "You are the faithful," he is quoted as saying, "and I am your commander. Therefore call me 'commander of the faithful'" (*amir al-mu'minin*). This indeed became the major formal title of the caliphs throughout the duration of that institution.

In medieval times, the caliph was the supreme sovereign of the Islamic empire, the head both of the religion and the state. The decline of religious authority and the increasing role of the military led to the emergence of a new kind of authority, the wielders of which were known first as *amir* and then as *sultan* (see pp. 180, 219). As the power of the sultans increased, the prestige and authority of the caliphs declined, and they became little more than figureheads exercising a nominal religious suzerainty over the real rulers.

For Sunni Muslims, the various dynasties of caliphs, in their time, were the legitimate heads of the Muslim state and community. For the Shi'a Muslims, these caliphs were usurpers, who had taken the place that rightfully belonged to the descendants of the Prophet. In the 10th century CE, a branch of the Isma'ili Shi'a established a caliphal dynasty of their own, known as the Fatimids, that is, the descendants of Fatima, the daughter of the Prophet. After coming to power in North Africa, they were able to conquer Egypt, and for a while to rule Syria, Palestine, and much of Arabia, offering a major threat to the Sunni caliphs in Baghdad. But eventually their regime collapsed, leaving the caliph in Baghdad with no serious rival to challenge him.

But there were other, greater dangers. When the Mongol invaders conquered Iraq and suppressed the Abbasid caliphate in Baghdad in 1258 CE, they laid to rest the ghost of an institution that was already dead. A refugee from the Abbasid caliphal family fleeing Baghdad was received in Cairo by the Sultan of Egypt, who found it opportune to establish a sort of puppet caliphate, with a purely nominal religious authority, while the sultan remained the real and effective head of the state. A line of such pseudo-caliphs, descended from the Abbasids, was maintained by the sultans of Egypt until 1517 CE, when the country was conquered by the Ottomans. According to Ottoman tradition, the last of the Abbasid caliphs of Cairo transferred his title and authority to the Ottoman sultan Selim whose descendants thus claimed to be the legitimate successors of the classical caliphate. In time, caliphal titles and prerogatives were claimed and exercised by many Muslim rulers—each, so to speak, a caliph in his own realm.

The idea of a genuine all-Islamic caliphate was revived by the Ottomans in the late 18th and 19th centuries and had some impact in the Muslim world, especially, for a while, among the Muslim minority in British-ruled India. The Ottoman caliphate, however, never won general acceptance and was finally abolished by the Turkish Republic in 1924. Since then, several Muslim rulers and leaders have flirted with the idea of a claim to the caliphate, but none has so far pursued it seriously. In one of his writings, Osama bin Ladin refers with obvious anguish to the "shame and humiliation" from which the Muslim world has suffered since the suppression of the caliphate and suggests that the time has come for its revival and renewal.

Opposition to Government in Islam

From the beginning, the reported events of Islamic history, supporting and supported by the precepts of Islamic tradition and law, express two distinct and indeed in a sense contradictory principles, one of them activist, the other quietist. The quietist principle has usually been dominant in Islamic states and societies, and for that reason, among others, is the better documented and studied. But the activist—one might even say, radical—tradition is also old, deep-rooted, and acquiring a new significance today.

Any inquiry in early Islamic history, based on the Islamic sources which purport to preserve the record of the early, formative events and ideas, must take into account two major developments, which have dominated recent scholarship devoted to this period. One of them is the growing skepticism among modern scholars as to the authenticity, even the historicity of the early Islamic historical narratives; the other is the tendency to see the advent of Islam not so much as a discontinuity, an abrupt change and a new beginning, but rather—in many aspects at least—as a continuation, admittedly in new forms and to some extent in new directions, of trends which can be traced to a remote, pre-Islamic past.

Both approaches must obviously affect an inquiry into early Islamic political attitudes, but neither need invalidate conclusions based on the examination of early and indeed later Islamic materials. Scholars have argued, with varying degrees of plausibility, that the earliest Arabic historical narratives are not historical at all, but are later creations, designed and assembled; according to some, to furnish a background of case law for subsequent jurisprudence, according to others, to provide a retroactive legitimization for later political structures and religious doctrines.

ISLAMIC HUMOR

One day, Sultan Mahmud of Ghazna (reigned 999-1030 CE) was hungry, and his servant brought him a dish of eggplant. He enjoyed it and said: "Eggplant is an excellent dish." The courtier who was with him immediately began to praise the eggplant with great eloquence.

But when the sultan had had enough of the eggplant, he said: "On the other hand, the eggplant is limited, even boring…" where upon the courtier began to denounce the limitations and monotony of the eggplant.

"What is this?" asked the Sultan. "A moment ago, you were praising the eggplant; now you are condemning it. What is this?"

"Your Majesty," said the courtier, "I am your courtier, not the eggplant's courtier."

For the history of attitudes and ideas, the literal accuracy of the narrative is of secondary importance. The narrative as preserved and studied contains what Muslims perceived to be their past, and it was this past, handed down in differing and sometimes contrasting versions, which shaped their ideas and was used by them to justify their actions. In a religion as political as Islam, in a polity as religious as the caliphate, such questions as the source and nature of authority, the obligation and limits of obedience, the definitions of legitimacy and usurpation, of justice and tyranny, and the manner of dealing with a tyrant or usurper, acquired a central importance. And in formulating and answering these questions, the narrative of early Islamic times, as transmitted to later Islamic times, furnished ample if sometimes contradictory guidance. So, too, did the fading memories of a more distant past surviving in a disguised or attenuated form after the advent of Islam. From the Judeo-Christian scriptures and memories came the notion of a Prophet who rebukes an unjust ruler, and of a Messiah who will come at the end of time to establish a more perfect order. From the Greco-Roman world came interesting arguments and stories about the theory and practice of tyrannicide. And from pre-Islamic Persia came distant but dangerous memories of religiously formulated opposition to authority, of revolutionary movements which challenged at once the religious, political, and social basis of the existing order, with a religious doctrine as ideology and a sect as instrument.

In a sense, the advent of Islam itself was seen as a revolution. It began, during the early career of the Prophet, as a challenge to the old leadership and the old order in Mecca. Its success overthrew and supplanted both, the one by the Prophet and his companions, the other by Islam—not just a religion in the limited, modern Western sense of that word, but rather in Islamic terms, that is, a new political, social, and cultural order, differing in many significant aspects from the old.

The prophet Muhammad, according to the traditional narrative, began his career in Mecca as an opposition leader and, for some time, was engaged in a struggle against authority as established among his people and in his birthplace. When his position became untenable, he moved to Medina, where he formed a government and, from this external base, finally accomplished the forcible overthrow and supersession of the old order at home.

In this supersession, as in all else, the Prophet is seen as the model and pattern of behavior. This pattern of resistance, migration, and return became a paradigm for Islamic leaders and movements which sought to challenge the existing order and establish a new one in its place. It was followed by many political-religious leaders. Some of them—like the Abbasids who came to Iraq via eastern Persia in the mid-8th century CE and founded Baghdad; the Fatimids, who came to Egypt via North Africa in the 10th century CE and founded Cairo; and the Ayatollah Khomeini, who returned to Iran via France in the late 20th century CE and founded the Islamic republic—were successful. Many others, in the course of fourteen centuries of Islamic history, tried and failed. There will surely be more.

The quietest tradition is classically grounded in the Koranic text: "Obey God, obey His Prophet, and those who hold authority among you" (4:59). It is amply documented in tradition and jurisprudence. According to this doctrine, obedience—even to the most improbable authority—is a religious duty as well as a political necessity, and disobedience is, therefore, a sin as well as a crime. "Obey whoever is placed in authority over you," says an early tradition, "even a flat-nosed Ethiopian slave"—stating the ultimate improbability in physical, racial, and social terms. "Tyranny is better than anarchy," says another tradition, providing a rationale for submission to authority, however oppressive it may be.

ISLAMIC HUMOR

The Caliph al-Mansur, addressing the rebellious population of Damascus, said to them: "You should praise God that he has given you me as your ruler. Since I started to rule, God has removed the plague which had been afflicting you."

A Bedouin who was present replied: "Allah indeed is merciful. He would not inflict both you and the plague upon us at the same time."

Resistance or even opposition to authority is designated mostly by words with a negative connotation. But the activist tradition too is based on Koranic texts, notably on the injunctions not to obey a variety of ancient and pagan tyrants. Thus, for example, in 18:28: "...and keep thy soul content with those who call on their Lord morning and evening, seeking his face; and let not thine eyes pass beyond them, seeking the pomp and glitter of this life; nor obey any whose heart we have permitted to neglect the remembrance of us, one who follows his own desires, whose case has gone beyond all bounds"; or, in 26:150–152: "But fear God and obey me and do not follow the bidding of those who are extravagant, who make mischief in the land, and do not mend (their ways)." These passages are confirmed and clarified by many hadiths, of which the most commonly cited quotes the Prophet as saying that "there is no obedience in sin" that is, when the ruler commands something which is sinful, the duty of obedience lapses. Some go even further and claim that it is replaced by a duty of disobedience.

There is a positive as well as a negative term for such action. A revolution which fails and is condemned is called *fitna*, a word meaning test or trial. A revolution which succeeds and brings about a change in the regime was called *dawla*, a word which originally meant "rotation" or "turn," and eventually came to mean state and dynasty. The Western term revolution, with the same primary meaning, has now undergone a similar transformation in the modern Middle East.

The fifty plus states that make up the Muslim world may be divided into three categories, depending on the type of regime by which they are ruled and the manner in which that regime is maintained. The first of these are regimes, usually traditional and established, that depend on loyalty for support and survival. This loyalty may be tribal, dynastic, regional, or sectarian. Obvious examples of the present day are the kingdom of Morocco and many of the emirates and sheikhdoms of the Arabian peninsula, such as Oman.

The second group are those whose basic demand from their subjects is not loyalty but obedience, enforced and maintained by a variety of repressive regimes. Many of these regimes describe themselves as revolutionary, the most widely accepted title to legitimacy in the Middle East at the present time. Their revolutions are presented in various forms, mostly in terms imported from the West. Regimes of this kind have no roots in Islamic history or culture. They are an importation from Europe and date especially from the periods first of Nazi, then of Soviet influence. The same, unfortunately, remains true of most of the former Soviet provinces that are now independent Muslim republics. More recently, in Iran, a new type of dictatorship has emerged, expressed in Islamic theocratic terms, but no less alien to Islamic political traditions, and no less influenced by the darker European examples.

Finally, there is a small but growing group of governments that rely not simply on loyalty or obedience, but try to achieve some measure of participation—in other words, of democracy. Democratic institutions, like fascist dictatorships, were an imitation of European practice—sometimes in emulation of European models, sometimes at the behest of European imperial overlords, as in the British and French mandatory regimes in Iraq and Syria. Most of these experiments failed and ended in coup d'etat or civil war, in either case culminating in dictatorship.

But not all of them failed. The first working democracy in an Arab country was in Lebanon, where the various communities, despite their often sharp differences, managed to cooperate in a reasonably functioning democratic system. It was ended not through any fault of the Lebanese but through the quarrels of their neighbors—first Palestinians, followed by Israelis and Syrians—spilling onto Lebanese soil.

Another experiment was the Turkish Republic, established in 1923. This might be called a quasi-democracy—one more of form than of substance—until the year 1946, when for the first time the country held a free and fair election. In a second free election in 1950, the government was defeated and smoothly transferred power to the victorious opposition. Since then, the Turkish Republic has gone through some difficulties but continues to function in a more or less democratic way to the present time. The reelection with a clear parliamentary majority of a government and party with an Islamist agenda will demonstrate how far such an agenda is or is not compatible with Western-style parliamentary democracy.

Finally, there is the attempt to develop a form of democratic government in Iraq. Great efforts are being made both to ensure and to prevent its achievement. Much will depend, in the Islamic world and far beyond, on the success or failure of these efforts.

Unmar said to Salman: "Am I a king or a Caliph?" And Salman answered: "If you have levied from the lands of the Muslims one dirham, or more, or less, and applied it unlawfully, you are a king, not a Caliph." And Umar wept.

—The Arab historian Al-Tabari (died 923 CE)

CHAPTER 9

The Wider World of Islam

In the preceding chapters, attention has been focused mainly on those regions of Southwest Asia and Northern Africa that in the late 19th and early 20th centuries came to be known as the Near East, then the Middle East, and are now frequently combined in "the Near and Middle East."

There are good reasons for this emphasis, both historical and contemporary. It was in this region that the Islamic faith, and after it, the Islamic community, state, and civilization, first arose and became a major force in human history, contributing to it in every significant field of human endeavor.

The Middle East has always been and still remains for Muslims, wherever they may be, the birthplace and center of their faith, toward which they turn in prayer every day, to which they travel in pilgrimage, and from which they draw guidance and inspiration in matters of religion, in the very wide Islamic interpretation of that term.

Even in what Westerners would regard as secular matters outside religious concern, the Middle East remains a powerful, though dwindling, force in other parts of the Muslim world. Of the three major languages spoken by Middle Eastern Muslims, Arabic and Persian are the scriptural and classical languages of Islamic civilization, with an importance comparable to that once enjoyed by Latin and Greek in Christendom. Turkish could not be described as either scriptural or classical, but was the dominant political language of the Islamic world for many centuries. Languages of the Turkic family are still spoken in various parts of the Islamic world and notably in the Muslim territories of the former Soviet Union.

The modern age has added a new component to Middle Eastern centrality—namely oil. A significant portion of the oil resources of the entire world are located in the Middle East and some immediately adjoining areas in Central Asia and Africa. The discovery and exploitation of this resource is entirely a European and American achievement, but in our own day, it has given new importance to the region and new and immense power to the governments that rule it and control those resources. In time, oil will either be exhausted or superseded as a source of energy; but in the meantime, it brings wealth, influence, and power to a diversity of Middle Eastern rulers and factions.

Mention should also be made of the strategic importance of the region, situated at the intersection of Asia, Africa, and Europe, with territorial bases in all three. In significant other respects, however, this region is ceasing to be the heartland and center of the Islamic world. Middle Eastern Muslims, by their very success in spreading and promoting their religion, have brought about a situation in which they have become a minority in the larger Islamic world which they did so much to create.

Since early times, the Islamic faith, and with it the Islamic culture, have spread in all directions at various times and in various ways—by conquest, by commerce, by conversion, and at some times and in some places, including our time, by migration.

The advance of Islam into Central Asia began with the first Arab conquerors and was continued by their successors, notably the Muslim Turks. The same is true of India, where a succession of Islamic invasions and conquests culminated in the creation of the Islamic empire of the Moguls, ruling the greater part of the Indian subcontinent from the 16th to the 18th centuries. Central and South Asia remained politically part of the Islamic world, until Islamic rule was replaced by European rule—the Russians in Central Asia and the British in India.

The spread of Islam to Southeast Asia was similar in some respects, different in others. Malaysia and Indonesia were never part of the great Islamic empires of the Middle East. Their incorporation into the Islamic world came about rather through peaceful processes—by commerce, influence, and conversion. Certainly there were local conflicts at times between Islamized rulers and their non-Islamized neighbors, but in general, the Islamization of this region may be described as peaceful. In the early modern age, Southeast Asia suffered the same fate as much of the rest of the non-Western world and was divided between the European empires, particularly the British and the Dutch. The departure of the Western imperial rulers left a number of Muslim states in the region, as well as Muslim minorities in some non-Muslim countries.

The spread of Islam in Africa followed a somewhat different pattern, with different results. The first Arab conquerors and their Turkish successors showed little interest in invading tropical Africa, and there too the spread of Islam was mainly by commerce—especially the slave trade—and conversion. The Sahara Desert seems to have been a more formidable obstacle than the Mediterranean Sea, and to this day, Muslim North Africa, in many respects, has more in common with Christian southern Europe than with Muslim sub-Saharan Africa.

As these vast new lands were added to the Islamic realm, new languages evolved, derived from the ancient languages of these peoples, transformed by the impact of Islam, its scriptures and its classics, in the way that the languages of pagan Europe were transformed by the Christian and Greco-Roman heritages. There are many such languages. Obvious examples are Swahili and Haussa in eastern and western Africa; Urdu in Pakistan and among the Muslim minority in India; Malay and Indonesian in Southeast Asia. Many of these Asian and African Muslim communities share a language with their non-Muslim compatriots, but they write it in the Arabic script with a significant vocabulary of Arabic loan words.

The largest Muslim populations at the present time are found in two areas, South Asia and Southeast Asia. In 1947, British India was partitioned into two states, one of them called Pakistan, a new term meaning "land of the pure," a Muslim majority state consisting of two separated parts, one on the western, the other on the eastern side of the subcontinent. Later, East Pakistan, as it was then called, broke away and became a separate independent state named Bangladesh. Even after the separation of these two Muslim majority areas, a significant Muslim minority remained in India, now one of the largest Muslim communities in the world.

With the ending of Dutch imperial rule in Southeast Asia, a new independent republic emerged, with the name of Indonesia, consisting primarily of the islands of Java and Sumatra, together with some smaller islands. The former British possessions in Malaya and some adjoining areas now form the predominantly Muslim state of Malaysia.

Between them, the Muslims of South and Southeast Asia number many hundreds of millions, far outnumbering the older Muslim centers in the Middle East. These Muslim states, notably Pakistan, have already begun to exercise considerable intellectual and, increasingly, political influence in the older centers of the Islamic world.

Today there are also large and rapidly growing Muslim communities in non-Muslim countries, some consisting of groups of Muslims left behind after the retreat of the Muslim powers from the countries that they had formerly conquered and ruled, others due to a phenomenon without precedent in history, the voluntary migration of Muslims from Muslim to non-Muslim countries.

These new communities, already growing rapidly by migration and demography, also increase their numbers by conversion. This happens in several ways, chiefly by intermarriage, and, also to an increasing extent, by active missionary propaganda. Conversion is particularly effective among minority groups with a grievance and a sense of being victims of discrimination, such as African Americans in the United States.

There is another important distinction to be made between two groups among the Muslim minorities abroad, some defined only by religion, others by both religion and ethnicity. Some are purely religious minorities, ethnically and linguistically indistinguishable from the majority. The most important example of these is the greater part of the Muslim minority in India. Another example is some, but not all, of the Muslim minorities in Balkan Europe. In contrast, many of the Muslim minorities in non-Muslim lands differ from the majority not only in religion but also in ethnicity and even language—for example, the Turks in Germany. This, of course, makes the related problems of assimilation and acceptance more difficult.

An important factor affecting the possibility of assimilation is the nature of identity in the host society. To become an American requires a change of political allegiance, and American society has a long history of facilitating this change. To become a Frenchman or a German requires a change of ethnic identity. This is obviously more difficult both for the immigrant and for the host societies. For a religion as political as Islam, issues of identity and loyalty are of major importance.

The resulting problems are being aggravated at the present time by the new waves of militant fundamentalism that are convulsing much of the Muslim world. Curiously, these movements are often more radical and more dangerous among the Muslim minorities in Europe and America than in the Muslim countries. There are several reasons for this. One is the new and unprecedented challenge of being a minority subject to the rule of an infidel government—for most of them, a new and painful experience. Another complicating factor is that whereas Muslim governments in Muslim countries have the experience, knowledge, and capacity to deal with movements of this kind, Western governments lack all of these and are moreover constrained by their own standards of tolerance and coexistence.

CHAPTER 10

Islam and the Economy

There is a view, widely held and occasionally expressed, according to which there is some fundamental incompatibility between Islam and the economy—that Islamic beliefs and practices are somehow obstructive to economic development and progress.

Two arguments are usually advanced in support of this view. The first is the Islamic ban on interest. Some have argued that the Arabic term *riba*, usually translated "interest," really means usury, that is, excessive interest. This view, however, has in the past commanded little or no acceptance among Muslims, though it enjoys some limited support at the present time. The jurists and theologians of Islam are virtually unanimous in rejecting this escape clause. Riba, they agree, means any interest, whether high or low. There is even a saying attributed to the Prophet that "to make money from money is evil." So, the argument goes, a strict enforcement of the ban on lending or borrowing money with interest would make any kind of modern finance—and, therefore, economic development—impossible.

The other argument adduced by those who claim that there is a fundamental incompatibility between Islam and economic development is the present state of most of the Islamic world, compared with other parts of the world, not only Europe and America, but also Asia, notably such spectacularly successful recent arrivals to modernity as South Korea.

There can be no doubt that the economic condition of much of the Islamic world, compared with other regions, is bad. This is grimly illustrated, exemplified, and documented in a series of reports on human development in the Arab lands, prepared by a committee of Arab intellectuals and published under the auspices of the United Nations. The picture they represent can only be described as appalling. It shows, for example, that the exports of the entire Arab world, other than oil, amount to less than those of Finland—one single European country of some five million inhabitants. The committee cited many other examples of equally startling disparities. A similar point is sometimes made by comparing the post-imperial history of former imperial dependencies—for example, of independent India and Pakistan, into which the British Indian Empire was partitioned, and of former British crown colonies such as Aden and Singapore. The contrasts are indeed striking.

Is there then some innate incompatibility between Islam and economic development? This question may be examined in two different ways:

1. By looking at Muslim scripture, tradition, theology, and law and seeing how they deal with economic matters
2. By looking at the economic record of the Islamic world in earlier times, when one might say that the society was more Islamic, not less Islamic than it is now, when Islam was still new, fresh, and more vigorous

As noted earlier, interest is forbidden. But profit on the other hand is not only permitted; it is praised, even extolled, in many of the hadiths, sayings attributed to the Prophet: "The best of gain is from honorable trade and from a man's work with his own hands"—in other words, commerce and manual labor; "To seek lawful gain is the duty of every Muslim"; another saying goes even further: "To seek lawful gain is a kind of jihad"; more remarkably: "The honest, truthful Muslim merchant will stand with the martyrs on the Day of Judgment."

These are just a few examples from a large number of hadiths. Some are more specific and explicit: "Only God can fix prices"—a very interesting observation. Many governments since remote antiquity have tried to fix prices and have usually found it difficult if not impossible. In the Islamic world, there were nearly always two precious metals in circulation: gold and silver, and prices were determined to a large extent by the exchange rates of gold and silver to each other as well as by the supply and demand of the actual commodities.

Turning from doctrine to practice, to the actual historical record, one must again come to the conclusion that during the great age of Islam, in what in European history is called the medieval period, the dominant culture was extremely conducive to economic development. In production—for example, agriculture and manufacturing—several products which were later of major importance in Western economic development first came to the West either from or through the Islamic world. Some originated there; others were imported from farther east, usually from India or China, developed to an unprecedented degree in the Islamic world and then passed on to the West.

The same is true of some other techniques and procedures. Examples of both are paper and numbers. Paper, as far as we know, was first manufactured in China and became known to the Arabs when they captured some Chinese paper-makers in central Asia in the mid-8th century. They immediately realized the importance of this product and began to manufacture and export paper on a large scale. This became a major element in economic development, particularly when linked with another importation from the East—positional, decimal numbers. This system was, it seems, invented in India. When the Muslims first went to the subcontinent, they saw its potential and immediately adopted and developed it in the Islamic world. From there, this system of notation passed to the Western world, where it came to be known as "Arabic numerals."

The combination of paper and numbers—both unknown in the Greco-Roman world—developed into something of immense economic importance, namely accountancy—accounts, records, banking—none of which would have been possible without them. Imagine trying to keep accounts in Roman numerals on parchment or clay tablets.

But interest is forbidden by Islam, and how could there be banking without interest? Already in the Middle Ages, many ways to solve this problem were found and, in time, a system of Islamic banking was developed which is widely used, particularly in Arabia. The basic principle of Islamic banking is risk-sharing: I don't lend you $1,000.00 at a rate of interest; I invest $1,000.00 in your enterprise. I take a share of your profit or suffer a share of your loss. This was the basic principle, and on the whole, is seems to have worked fairly well. When it goes bad, as it sometimes does, it is for reasons other than any inherent flaw in the system. During the Middle Ages, the Muslim world developed a very elaborate system of banking and credit. By the 9th century CE, for example, a merchant could draw a check in Iraq and cash it in Morocco. There is considerable evidence of a system of international credit and banking without precedent in antiquity. This, of course, along with much else, was passed to the Western world, where it became a major component in the subsequent economic development of Europe and its overseas settlements and colonies.

There is an interesting linguistic trail left on the route from East to West. "Check"—a piece of paper on which you write a figure and sign your name—is a Persian word that came to the West via Arabic. *Douane*, the French word for customs administration, is the Arabic term *diwan* (see p. 189). "Sugar," unknown in the Greco-Roman world, is a Persian word. According to one school of thought, sugar originated in Persia; according to another, sugar originated in China and came via Persia. The words that we use, however, are unequivocally Persian. In the Persian language, sugar is variously known as *sheker* and *cand*—sugar candy, in other words. Coffee originally came from Ethiopia, probably from the district of Kaffa, where it grows wild and where the intricate and complex transformation of a wild bean into a hot drink was first devised. From Ethiopia it was taken to the Yemen in the 15th century, and then northward along both sides of the Red Sea to Arabia, Egypt, Syria, and Turkey. Both coffee and sugar became major items of export from the Islamic Middle East to Europe.

For sale in the Spice Market of the Grand Bazaar, Istanbul, Turkey.
(© Carson Ganci/Design Pics/CORBIS All Rights Reserved)

For a long time, Western Europe, like sub-Saharan Africa, was seen as an outer wilderness beyond the frontiers of civilization, from which nothing of any value could be imported, except raw materials and slaves.

All this makes the subsequent change the more puzzling and poses the questions that the peoples of the Islamic world have been asking themselves, with increasing anguish, for centuries. What went wrong? How did the previously ignorant barbarians of the European wilderness begin to develop more powerful states and armies, based on more advanced and sophisticated economies, while the peoples of the Islamic world fell back from the position they had held for centuries in the forefront of world civilization, to a condition of stagnation or, worse, deterioration, leading inevitably to subordination?

To some extent, this changed relationship was due to developments in the West. Notable among these was the discovery of the Americas. This gave the Europeans a new and plentiful source of precious metals, which significantly changed the commercial relationship between the Christian and Muslim worlds. It also gave the Christian powers control of tropical and sub-tropical territories, in which they were able to grow, at lower cost, crops which they had previously imported from the East. Notable among these were coffee and sugar. By the 18th century, when a Turk or an Arab allowed himself that typical Middle Eastern indulgence, a cup of sweetened coffee, the chances were that both the coffee and the sugar had been grown in European overseas colonies in Asia and America and bought from European merchants at significantly lower prices than the local product. Only the hot water was of local provenance, and in the course of the 19th century, even that ceased to be true, as services and utilities were taken over by European companies.

But the changed relationship was also facilitated and indeed accelerated by certain internal difficulties, notably by the absence of two distinguishing features of the Western economies—competition and innovation.

ISLAMIC HUMOR

The devil was asked: "Which group of people do you love most?"
He replied: "The market-brokers."
They asked him why, and he answered: "Not only do they speak falsehood, which in itself delights me, but they swear to it as well."

In the typical Middle Eastern market, the makers and sellers of goods are grouped in guilds, usually in the same place. All the bakers are in one street and charge more or less the same price for the same loaf. All the shoemakers are on another street and provide identical products and services. There is no competition. On the contrary, the system is designed to eliminate competition. The result is a way of life that is very decent, very humane, very gentlemanly. If one of them is not doing well or is known to have problems, his colleagues will direct customers to him and generally attempt to seek a fair distribution. From the human point of view, it is an admirable system; from the economic point of view, it is a catastrophic system in that it eliminates or minimizes competition and, therefore, all the motives for improvement and invention. This lack of competition, compared with the cutthroat competition of the European merchants, was probably one of the main reasons why European trade advanced so rapidly at the expense of Middle Eastern traders.

Market in Damascus, Syria.
(Richard Ross/Image Bank/Getty Images)

The custom, familiar to visitors to the souks and bazaars, of bargaining over prices is not really a form of competition—rather an elaborate social ritual, normally understood by both sides. Sometimes, when an ignorant visitor agrees and pays too high a price, the disconcerted merchant returns more than the appropriate amount of change.

Carpets for sale.

Connected with the lack of competition is another deficiency—the lack of innovation. With this kind of guild system, with manufacturers and merchants not competing but doing the same thing, in the same way, at the same price, there is little or no incentive to devise new and better methods. Change in itself becomes suspect.

There is a religious dimension to this. In Islamic usage, the word *bid'a*, literally "innovation," has a negative connotation. Tradition is sacred; novelty is suspect. The possibility of a good innovation is admitted, in which case it is designated as such. The Arabic term is *bid'a hasana*. But unless it is specifically described as good, an innovation is presumed to be bad. And that is not conducive to economic development.

Another important factor is the absence, shortage, or dwindling of certain resources, certain raw materials. Probably the most important of these is wood. Western travelers in the Middle East cannot but be struck by the absence of wood and, therefore, of things made of wood.

This can be seen in housing, transportation, and many other aspects. Where wood is rare or costly, one does not use it for such base purposes as carts, but for more exalted purposes. Not surprisingly, Middle Eastern artists developed a beautiful and sophisticated art of woodwork. But the wheeled cart, the basis of transportation in other parts of the world, was virtually unknown in the Middle East. Travelers from the Middle East to both east and west, in both Asia and Europe, often write with wonderment about the wheeled cart, something outside their experience. Its absence from the society clearly had a very negative effect on the development of commerce.

The same may be said, perhaps to a lesser extent, of ships. Ships were, for the most part, made of wood and, therefore, were few and small. Middle Eastern states did not go in for extensive shipping as did the Chinese and more recently the Europeans. Also, ships that were built to face the Atlantic were obviously different from ships built for the Mediterranean or the Red Sea. The Atlantic ship was better for both commerce and war, and its use enabled even small European countries like Holland and Portugal to build great empires in the East. Even the mightiest of the Eastern empires had nothing that could stand up to a well-armed Portuguese galleon.

These ships totally changed the balance of power, not only militarily, but also commercially, because they were faster, cheaper, and safer than anything available until then. By the 18th century, even Muslim pilgrims going from Indonesia to the holy cities in Arabia booked their passage on European ships. The same problem arose on land as well as at sea. Since wheeled vehicles were rare and expensive, and Middle Easterners did not, therefore, develop cars or trains as did the Europeans, they once again fell behind in transportation. This gave the West an immense economic advantage.

Another problem in the Arab world was the camel—both a blessing and a curse. The camel is an extraordinarily efficient mode of transportation, vastly superior to the horse, donkey, or any other pack animal. The camel can travel great distances without refueling, so to speak, and can carry enormous loads. The camel thus removed the incentive which people might otherwise have had to devise and develop new methods of transportation. In a sense, the camel was the ancient and medieval equivalent of oil, the discovery and exploitation of which has been a similar blessing and curse for much of the Middle East today.

Another important factor in the rise and spread of Western power was the commercial corporation, the predecessor of the limited or incorporated company of our day. The great European commercial corporations, operating both at home and abroad, at the same time ensured both cooperation within the group and competition against other groups. The concept of the corporate entity in the Western world goes back a long way, to Roman and even Greek times. The most important example was the city, the member of which was the citizen. The city was a legal entity in itself: It could own property; it could buy and sell; it could sue and be sued. All this helped to prepare the way for the great commercial corporations of later times. This did not happen in the Islamic world. In the Greco-Roman sense, there was no city—just an accumulation of urban habitations. What was really important was not so much the city as the neighborhood or quarter, this being usually either tribal or occupational, or some combination of the two. This helped sustain the guild system and obstruct the development of great commercial and industrial corporations, Western-style.

There is another factor, dating back to remote antiquity, affecting the economic development—or lack of development—of the region. The oldest economies in the Middle East were river-valley societies, two in particular, Egypt and Iraq, the valleys of the Nile and of the Tigris and Euphrates rivers. These were the two most ancient centers of civilization in the region and indeed in the world. Lacking rainfall, their agriculture depended on irrigation, which in turn needed to be maintained by a system of canals, with engineers and workers to construct and operate them, and bureaucrats to administer the engineers and workers. This developed into a kind of centralized administration, with bureaucratic control. For a long time, this was an advantage, even a necessity. Eventually, it became a serious impediment, compared with the freer and more open economies of the Western world, where the farmer depended on rainfall from heaven and was, therefore, less subservient to earthly authority.

Perhaps the most important economic factor in the modern Middle East is oil. This has been a blessing, in that it has provided ample revenues. It has also been a curse, in that it made it unnecessary for these societies to embark on economic development and thus enabled them to avoid the political consequences of such development. All Americans are familiar with the slogan: "No taxation without representation." What we sometimes forget is that the converse is also true: No representation without taxation. Middle Eastern rulers with oil wealth at their disposal do not need to levy taxes from their own people. They, therefore, do not need to have elected assemblies help them in that process. This gives them power over their subjects without parallel in societies where governments depend on subjects both able and ready to pay taxes. Oil wealth has sometimes also made it possible to give enormous power and influence to what otherwise might have been marginal fringe groups. The power and influence of the Wahhabis in Saudi Arabia, and from there in much of the Islamic world, is an obvious example.

Dubai business skyline.

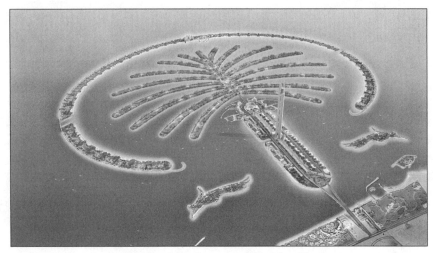

Palm Jumairah artifical islands, Dubai, constructed for affluent property owners.
(© Al-Nakheel/CORBIS All Rights Reserved)

Another problem was the low esteem in which trade and traders came to be held in the post-classical period, in much though by no means all of the Muslim world. The higher ranks of society were the military, the bureaucrats, and the religious establishment, and effective political power was usually shared or disputed among these. With rare exceptions, notably the earlier period, merchants were held in low esteem, especially when, as often happened in late medieval and early modern times, those merchants were not Muslims but members of the religious minorities, Jews, and to an increasing extent, Christians, primarily of Eastern churches. The earlier respect accorded to merchants in the traditions of the Prophet seems to have been forgotten.

Another element, much discussed especially in more recent times, is that of corruption. This does not seem to have been an important issue in early times. It first becomes prominent in the 16th century and has been linked, not implausibly, with the inflow of American silver and later gold, and the consequent collapse of indigenous currencies. From then on, it seems to have become an inescapable part of the process of modernization and is rampant in modern times.

The modern "market"—a mall in Dubai.
(Mira.com/Peter, Georgina Bowater)

All societies, unfortunately, have their own distinctive forms of corruption, of mixing money and power. In the Western democracies, one makes money in the marketplace and then uses that money to buy power or, at least, access or influence. In much of the East today, the more usual sequence is to seize power, usually by force, and then use that power to acquire money. Morally, there would appear to be little to choose between the two methods, but the latter probably does more damage, both in politics and in the economy.

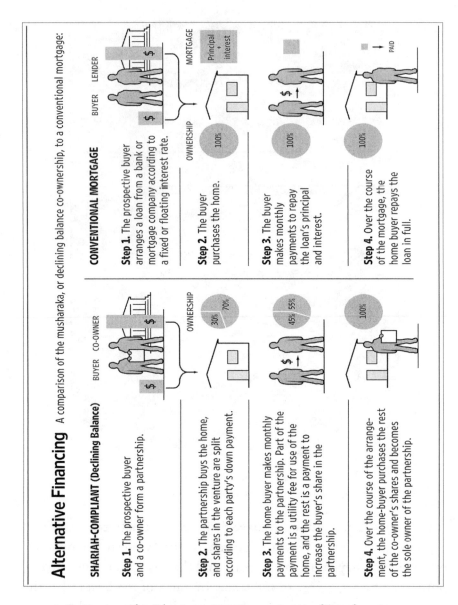

Alternative Financing   A comparison of the musharaka, or declining balance co-ownership, to a conventional mortgage:

SHARIAH-COMPLIANT (Declining Balance)

BUYER   CO-OWNER

OWNERSHIP

Step 1. The prospective buyer and a co-owner form a partnership.

Step 2. The partnership buys the home, and shares in the venture are split according to each party's down payment.

30% 70%

Step 3. The home buyer makes monthly payments to the partnership. Part of the payment is a utility fee for use of the home, and the rest is a payment to increase the buyer's share in the partnership.

45% 55%

Step 4. Over the course of the arrangement, the home-buyer purchases the rest of the co-owner's shares and becomes the sole owner of the partnership.

100%

CONVENTIONAL MORTGAGE

BUYER   LENDER

MORTGAGE

Principal + interest

OWNERSHIP

Step 1. The prospective buyer arranges a loan from a bank or mortgage company according to a fixed or floating interest rate.

Step 2. The buyer purchases the home.

100%

Step 3. The buyer makes monthly payments to repay the loan's principal and interest.

100%

Step 4. Over the course of the mortgage, the home buyer repays the loan in full.

100%

PAID

Comparison of an Islamic mortgage to a western, traditional mortgage.
("Mutual Interest: When Hedge Funds Meet Islamic Finance."
The Wall Street Journal, *Thursday, August 9, 2007.)*

CHAPTER 11

Women in Islam

In the course of the 19th century, Muslims were becoming more and more aware of the weakness and poverty of their world, compared with the rich, powerful, and advancing West. Among the Turks, Arabs, Persians, and other Muslim peoples, the debate began and grew with increasing anguish and intensity: "What have we done wrong? How can we put it right?"

Many diagnoses were offered, and appropriate remedies prescribed and applied, in a process that came to be known as "modernization."

At first and for a while, the diagnoses and, therefore, the prescriptions, were predominantly military, since it was on the field of battle that the problem was first seen in clear and unequivocal terms. But military reforms produced only bigger and better defeats, and Muslim reformers looked elsewhere, notably to various kinds of political reform and economic development. None proved very effective.

In 1867, a young Turkish writer named Namik Kemal published a magazine article suggesting a radically different approach. For him, the really important difference between the Islamic world and the West was their treatment of women, and it was this difference that was the main cause of the success of the one society and the comparative failure of the other. "Our women," he said, "are now seen as serving no useful purpose to mankind other than having children. They are considered simply as serving for pleasure, like musical instruments or jewels. But they constitute perhaps more than half of our species. Preventing them from contributing to the maintenance and improvement of others by means of their efforts infringes the basic rules of public cooperation to such a degree that our national society is stricken like a human body that is paralyzed on one side. Yet women are not inferior to men in their intellectual and physical capacities....The reason why women among us are thus deprived is the perception that they are totally ignorant and know nothing of right and duty, benefit and harm. Many evil consequences result from this position of women, the first being that it leads to a bad upbringing for their children." Namik Kemal's essay, despite his powerful argument and his striking metaphors, seems to have had only a limited impact at the time.

The advent of Islam brought a significant improvement to the position of women in ancient Arabia and to some extent in the neighboring countries. But in certain respects, the inferiority of women to men remained deeply rooted and amply documented in Muslim scripture, tradition, and law. Three examples may suffice. A woman's testimony as a witness is worth only half that of a man. This discrimination is documented in Koran 2:282: "Get two witnesses out of your own men, and if there are not two men, then a man and two women so that if one of them errs, the other can remind her." Another example is the compensation that is owed for killing a person: "The law of equality is prescribed to you in case of murder: the free for the free, the slave for the slave, the woman for the woman" (Koran 2:178). The laws regarding inheritance are equally specific: "If there are brothers and sisters, (they share), the male having twice the share of the female" (Koran 4:176). Muslim laws of inheritance are extremely complex, and sometimes vary as between Sunnis and Shi'a, and even between the various schools of Sunni law. But the basic principles are as set forth in the Koran.

Marriage

Similar principles apply in marriage, which is both a religious and legal institution in Islam, meticulously regulated by holy law. Conditions vary somewhat between the different schools of Islamic jurisprudence, in different parts of the Islamic world, and at different periods, but certain basic rules remain the same.

In a widely discussed and diversely interpreted passage, the Koran refers to the greater power and, therefore, greater responsibility of men in the protection and maintenance of women and authorizes husbands, in case of disloyalty or misconduct, to beat their wives (Koran 4:34). This verse has been variously interpreted, explained, and explained away.

In Islam, marriage is a contract agreed between the bridegroom and the legal guardian of the bride, who would normally be her nearest ascendant male relative. In the case of a freed slavewoman, the guardian would be the former owner who manumitted her, or his heir. If for some reason no guardian is available, one may be appointed by the public authority—the governor or the qadi. The jurists lay down that the guardian can only give the bride in marriage with her consent, but in the case of a virgin, silence may be taken as consent. A father or grandfather—but no other guardian—may give a virgin daughter or granddaughter in marriage without her consent, but the jurists impose a number of restrictions on this power to safeguard the interests of the bride.

There are several impediments to marriage, the most important being blood relationship, certain forms of foster relationship or relationship by marriage, and religion. A Muslim woman may in no circumstances marry a non-Muslim. A Muslim man, according to most schools of jurisprudence, may marry a woman of the permitted religions—in practice, Jewish or Christian. But the children would have to be brought up as Muslims. A woman is allowed only one husband, and the existence, therefore, of an undissolved previous marriage constitutes a total ban. A man is allowed up to four wives at any one time, and there can be no valid marriage with a fifth. The law does, however, allow concubinage, that is, the sexual use of female slaves.

A divorce is relatively simple and easy, but requires full recognition of the property rights of the divorced wife and restitution where necessary. A man can divorce his wife by simple repudiation (*talaq*), at his discretion. No reason or justification is required, but the circumstances are elaborately regulated in the Koran, which devotes a whole chapter to this topic (Koran 65; see also 2:228-232, 236-7, 241; 4:35). A wife cannot divorce her husband, but can appeal to a judge to order her husband to divorce her.

Shari'a law as interpreted by the Shi'a allows a form of marriage known as *mut'a*. This is a contract of marriage for a limited period of time, which may extend over years, or be as short as a single day. At the expiration of the period stated in the contract, the marriage is automatically dissolved. The relative positions of the spouses, and of any children resulting, are on the same basis as a normal marriage. This form of marriage was rejected by the Sunni jurists as a form of licensed prostitution; it was defended as a necessary provision for long journeys and long absences from home.

In many modern Muslim states, attempts have been made to reform the marriage laws by legislation, notably in restricting the discretionary power of divorce by repudiation and preventing the forced marriage of minors. In Iran, the government of the Shah raised the age of marriage for girls to 18; the Islamic revolution, which came to power in 1979, has lowered it to 9, the age of A'isha, the youngest of the Prophet's wives, when he consummated his marriage with her.

In Islamic law, the *mahr*, sometimes misleadingly translated as "dowry," is a kind of bridal gift given by the bridegroom to his bride, whose property it becomes. The mahr is an essential part of the contract of marriage, which is not valid without it. There are no specific rules as to the amount of the mahr, though some of the jurists lay down a minimum. The amount has, of course, varied according to time, place, and the married couple's circumstances. The mahr becomes the unchallengeable property of the wife, which she may use in any way that she chooses. If a man divorces his wife at any time after consummation, she is entitled to the mahr in full, with reimbursement for any part that has been used or spent by her husband. Islamic law and practice did indeed give married women, from the beginning, independent property rights unknown in the Western world until comparatively modern times. The reality of these property rights is attested by ample archival evidence, notably in the imperial Ottoman archives in Istanbul, showing that women did indeed own property and money, sometimes large fortunes, which they disposed at will.

The negative side of these laws was a strong inducement for a husband, wishing to divorce his wife, to accuse her of adultery, in which case her property and also her life were forfeit. Islamic law seeks to prevent misuse of this rule by laying down extremely elaborate conditions for the proof of a charge of *zina*, an Arabic term often translated "adultery" but, in fact, covering any unlawful sexual relationship. A similar mistranslation, this time from the Hebrew, occurs in the seventh of the Ten Commandments, forbidding adultery. The word used in the original text similarly denotes any form of illicit sexual activity.

The Koran lays down that, in cases of adultery or fornication, both the man and the woman guilty of the offense are to be flogged "with a 100 lashes.... Let no compassion move you in their case, in a matter ordained by God, if you believe in God and the last day" (Koran 24:2). The text goes on to require four eyewitnesses for adultery and to prescribe severe punishment for those who make false accusations.

These requirements for proof were not always observed and more often, in fact, were reversed. In general, however, women's property rights were respected, and a considerable number of pious endowments by women of property (see *Waqf*, p. 222) survived into modern times in many parts of the Islamic world.

While the Koran says that a man may have up to four wives at any one time, modern reformers point out that the text also says that a man must treat them equally, and they argue that since this is impossible, the text is, in effect, a commandment for monogamy. To this, both traditionalists and radicals reply, "God does not speak in riddles. If God meant one wife, God would say one wife."

The Koran is in fact quite explicit and permits "…two, three or four wives. But if you fear that you will not be able to treat them equally, then only one wife, or those whom your right hands own" (Koran 4:3). This last phrase is commonly understood to denote female slaves who may be used as concubines. They include women taken as booty in war. The rules of marriage and concubinage for the prophet are somewhat different and are set forth in Koran 33:50. According to his biographers, the Prophet left ten or eleven widows, as well as some slavewomen.

Generally, in the modern period, the practice of polygamy has been declining in the Muslim world, partly for economic reasons, perhaps more for social reasons, and the growing feeling that this is no longer in accord with present-day social thought and practice. The recent militant revival of Islamic traditionalism, and the accompanying growth of a new Islamic radicalism, have brought a new campaign by some Muslim clerics, mainly in Saudi Arabia, defending polygamy against its detractors.

Their arguments may be summarized as follows. Because of menstruation, women are unavailable sexually to their husbands for several days, sometimes as many as ten days, every month; they are unavailable for longer periods during pregnancy and childbirth. According to Islamic thought, since male sexual impulses are deemed to be stronger than those of women, it is impossible for a man to be satisfied with just one woman. In the Western world, the resulting need is met in two ways, by adultery and prostitution. Neither of these is decent or acceptable. The Muslim solution of polygamy is both, providing an outlet for male needs, and at the same time giving respectability to the women and legitimacy to any children that may result. Before the advent of Islam, there was no limit on the number of wives a man might have. Islam imposed a maximum limit of four. These arguments do not lack cogency if one accepts the underlying presumption—that the prime purpose of marriage is to satisfy male sexual needs.

IN DEFENSE OF POLYGAMY

Early in the 21ˢᵗ century, a leading Sunni Arab Sheikh, Yusuf al-Qarad-hawi, said: "There is no society without polygamy. Westerners who condemn and reject polygamy are doing it themselves. The difference between their polygamy and our polygamy is that theirs is immoral and inhuman. The man [in the West] sleeps with more than one woman, and if the second woman gets pregnant, he denies responsibility for the child and does not support the woman financially. It is nothing but lust."

Sheikh Taysir al-Tamimi said: "As everyone knows, in non-Islamic societies that prohibit polygamy, there are many lovers and mistresses alongside the wife. I say this to those who demand equality and whine about women's rights, that by permitting polygamy, Islam protects the woman's humanity and emotions and secures her right to marry and gain honor and esteem, instead of becoming a professional paramour lacking in rights whose children are thrown onto the garbage heap."

Slavery

The use of female slaves, including captives taken in jihad, as concu-bines was sanctioned by both law and custom. The offspring of such a union, if recognized as such by the father, was born free; the mother, according to the predominant view among the jurists, could not be sold and became free on her owner's death.

The deterioration of the position of women can be seen by compar-ing the historical narratives about rulers and other leading figures in the early and later centuries of Islam. In the earliest period, we know something about the wives and mothers of rulers. They were, for the most part, free Arab ladies and played some part in society and, there-fore, in the historical narrative. In the later era of the caliphs and sul-tans, we know virtually nothing about the women in their lives, except sometimes their mothers, a few of whom exercised some influence in the palace. Such interludes of feminine influence were seen as excep-tional and, more important, as reprehensible. Most of the sultans were the sons of nameless slave concubines.

In modern times, slavery has been legally abolished, and with it, concubinage, in most of the Muslim world (see *Slavery*, pp. 216-217).

Honor Killing and Mutilation

At a time when European opinion and comment were predominantly hostile to Islam, the great Hungarian Jewish orientalist Ignaz Goldziher devoted much time and effort to defending Islamic practice and achievements against detractors. A particularly important point he made was that Islam as a religion and as a culture should not be blamed for the tribal customs of some of the peoples who adopted it. A good example is the genital mutilation of young females, widely practiced in Africa and, to a lesser extent, in some other places, but without any foundation whatsoever in Islamic scripture, tradition, or law. Another example is the practice of honor killing.

Islamic legislation in the Koran and in the Shari'a is designed to protect women from abuse of this kind, but in many parts of the Islamic world today, even the rules of law designed to protect women are used to abuse them. When the Prophet's nine-year-old wife, A'isha, chatted briefly with a young boy during a journey, she was accused of adultery, which was punishable by death. The Prophet, following a revelation, ruled that such a charge had to be supported by four adult male witnesses. This rule, designed to protect women, is commonly used to protect their assailants and is interpreted to mean that a woman accusing anyone of an attack on her is required to produce the four adult male witnesses, which is highly unlikely. In present-day Western legal systems, a prime issue in judging an illicit sexual encounter is whether it is consensual or coerced. In Shari'a, this is not an issue. Instead, the prime issue is whether the relationship is lawful or unlawful. A lawful relationship can only occur between a man and a woman who is his wife or his slave concubine. Any other is unlawful. The popular, though not legal, presumption is that in such an unlawful relationship, it is the woman—even a child—who is the instigator, and in this sense the elaborate covering of the female face and body is designed not so much to protect women as to protect men from their incandescent sexuality.

There have been a number of attempts in recent years to legislate against honor killings. A draft law proposed by King Abdullah of Jordan, criminalizing honor killing, was rejected by the Jordanian parliament. Turkey, Egypt, and Pakistan have passed such laws, but public opinion has prevented their effective enforcement. It is difficult to get a conviction, and even with a conviction, it is unusual for the perpetrator to receive more than a nominal penalty.

Iranian women dressed in abayas, Shiraz, Iran.
(Getty Images)

Veiling

The wearing of the veil is now widely regarded as an essential part of the Islamic creed. It was not always so. In pre-Islamic Arabia, as far as we know, the veil was worn by married women of a certain rank, but not by women in general. With the advent and expansion of Islam, the custom of wearing the veil spread rapidly in Arabia and elsewhere and became normal for ladies in towns. It was not, however, generally adopted by the women of the nomads, peasants, and some of the urban lower classes. To some extent, this relative freedom continued through medieval into modern times. But in most of the Islamic world, veiling and, increasingly, the seclusion of women, became the norm.

A change began as part of the process of modernization in the 19th century. In about 1873, the ruler of Egypt founded the first school for girls, and some Egyptian women of the upper classes began to appear without a veil. The first serious attack on the veil was in a famous book titled *The Liberation of Woman*, published in 1899 and written by a young Egyptian lawyer named Qasim Amin, who had studied in Paris and acquired a French girlfriend. He became a passionate advocate of women's rights in the Muslim world. He was particularly concerned about the veil, which he described as "the vilest form of servitude." He was careful not to demand that the veil be abolished; rather that it should be used only in strict conformity with Islamic rules—and these, he argued, in no way justified the way in which women were treated in his day. His book began a debate—and a struggle—which have been going on ever since, in more and more regions of the Islamic world.

Banning the veil, a deeply entrenched custom, was not an easy matter, and even Kemal Atatürk, the founder of the Turkish republic, who legislated concerning men's costume and headgear, did not formally prohibit the veil, but tried, with considerable success, to eliminate it by education and propaganda. Khomeini, the leader and ideologist of the Iranian revolution of 1979, saw the emancipation of women as one of the most evil of the Shah's westernizing reforms and demanded a strict enforcement of the old rules concerning the seclusion of women and the concealment of their bodies (see *Abaya, Burqa, Chador,* and *Niqab* in "Terms and Topics").

Sunni woman in a veil called a niqab.

The struggle continues in much of the Muslim world today. It may be noted that the veil comes in a variety of forms, ranging from total concealment of head and body, with only small slits for the eyes (*niqab*), to a small piece of cloth covering only part of the face. Today, some kind of head or face covering is often worn, even by secular women, as a protection against groping, verbal taunts, and other forms of abuse in crowded public places.

Fully veiled women at their graduation ceremony.

Emancipation

The argument over women's dress was, of course, merely the outward expression of the much larger problem of the status of women in society. In the long run, it may yet prove that the emancipation of women is the most enduring and far-reaching change in Islamic society resulting from the long period of Western impact and influence. Certainly, it has been one of the major targets of the different schools of militant Islamic revival. From the traditional point of view, the emancipation of women—allowing them to reveal their faces, arms, and legs, and to mingle socially and in the workplace with men—is an incitement to immorality and promiscuity, and a deadly blow to the very heart of Islamic society, the Muslim family and home.

The emancipation of women came in a number of ways and was due to a variety of circumstances, most if not all of which can be attributed to European influence or example. The abolition of chattel slavery made concubinage illegal, and though it lingered on for some time in the remoter areas, it ceased to be either common or accepted. In a few countries, notably Turkey and, in effect if not in law, Tunisia, and Iran under the Shah, even polygamy was banned. In many other Muslim states, while still lawful, it was hemmed in by many restrictions and became socially unacceptable in the urban middle and upper classes, as well as economically impractical for the urban lower classes.

The economic position of women was relatively good under the traditional dispensation—certainly far better than that of women in most Christian countries before the adoption of modern legislation. Economic needs were of major importance in the emancipation of women. Peasant women had from time immemorial been part of the workforce and had, in consequence, enjoyed certain social freedoms denied to their sisters in the cities.

Economic modernization brought a need for female labor. This became a significant factor in the Ottoman Empire during the first World War, when, as a result of the adoption of the European device of conscription, most of the male population were in the armed forces. The social changes necessitated by economic involvement continued in the inter-war period and after, and even brought legislative changes in favor of women. These were of some consequences in social and family life. Education for women also made considerable progress, and by the 1970s and 1980s, considerable numbers of women were enrolled as students in the universities. They began in the so-called "women's professions" of nursing and teaching, traditional in Europe and gradually becoming so in the lands of Islam, but later they began to penetrate to other professions and careers. Even their enrollment in the traditional professions was too much for some of the militants. Khomeini spoke with great anger of what he saw as inevitable immorality resulting from the employment of women to teach adolescent boys.

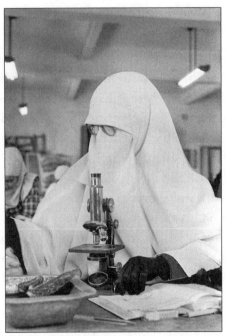

A fully veiled student in the biology department at Cairo University.
(Copyright Abbas /Magnum Photos)

The question of political rights is relatively unimportant in a region where, with few exceptions, the precarious parliamentary systems which once existed gave way to more or less autocratic governments, controlled by either the army or the party. Both are overwhelmingly male.

Westerners tend naturally to assume that the emancipation of women is part of liberalization, and that women will consequently fare better in liberal than in autocratic regimes. Such an assumption would be far from certain, and often the reverse is true. Among Arab countries, the legal emancipation of women went farthest in Iraq and South Yemen, both ruled by notoriously repressive regimes. It lagged behind in Egypt, among the more tolerant and open of Arab societies. It is in such societies that public opinion, still mainly male and mainly conservative, has the greatest influence. Women's rights have suffered the most serious reverses in countries where the fundamentalists have influence or, as in Iran, where they rule. Indeed, as already noted, the emancipation of women by modernizing rulers was one of the main grievances of the fundamentalists, and the reversal of this trend is in the forefront of their agenda.

Nevertheless, it is clear that irreversible changes have taken place and will continue. There is little likelihood of a restoration of concubinage in those places where it has been abolished, nor is it likely that there will be a return to polygamy among the educated classes in Middle Eastern cities. Fundamentalist influences have affected the content and manner of education for women, but, as the example of Iran suggests, this will not return them to their previous condition of ignorance. And while, in Islamic lands, as in the West in the past, there are significant numbers of women who speak and work against their own emancipation, the long-term trend must surely be for greater freedom. There are now great numbers of educated and emancipated, often Western-educated, women in Islamic lands, and they will have a powerful impact on the next generation.

ISLAMIC HUMOR

Ash'ab heard a certain woman of Medina pray and say: "O please God, do not let me die until you have forgiven my sins!"

And Ash'ab said to her: "You wicked woman! You are not asking God for forgiveness; you are asking Him for immortality."

Women's styles coexist on the beach in Morocco.
(Copyright Abbas / Magnum Photos)

CHAPTER 12

Dress

In a message to all humanity, the Koran states: "O children of Adam, we have given you clothing to cover your shame, and to be an adornment for you, but the garb of piety is the best" (7:26). The early Arab lexicographers add an obvious further purpose—"to protect against heat and cold." Common usage, sometimes backed by state enforcement, added yet another function for clothing—to proclaim identity and allegiance.

Some forms of clothing can be traced back in the Middle East to remote antiquity. The earliest and most basic are headgear and footwear, for protection against nature, and some form of girdle or loincloth, presumably for protection against one's fellow men. By the time of the advent of Islam in the 7th century CE, people in all the countries of the Middle East, including desert Arabia, had become accustomed to wearing voluminous clothing, covering most of their bodies.

The clothing of peasants and nomads varied little through the centuries. In the towns, there was far greater variety, reflecting changes in political domination and cultural influence. Fashion in the modern sense seems to have been unknown, but new dominant groups brought new styles of dress symbolizing their dominance. These groups came from different parts of the world; Turks and then Mongols from the East, Europeans and then Americans from the West. The modern phase was initiated by the adoption of European dress in the 19th century, first for men and then, more slowly and to a much more limited extent, for women. Headgear was particularly important as a badge of identity, because of its obvious relevance to Muslim worship. Long after the acceptance of jackets and trousers, Western-style hats and caps were rejected. More recently, even this barrier has been overcome, as more and more Muslims no longer engage in daily or even weekly prayer.

Dress as a mark of identity was sometimes proudly claimed, occasionally reluctantly accepted under constraint. From time to time, various medieval Muslim rulers required the Christians and Jews to wear special garments or headgear, so that they might be recognized at sight and not be mistaken for Muslims. In 1009 CE, an edict in Egypt even required Christians and Jews in the public bathhouse to retain a distinguishing emblem—a cross for Christians, a small bell for Jews. In general, however, such sartorial discrimination was exceptional, and the evidence is that even where these rules existed, they were not strictly enforced.

Some garments from the Islamic world were in various ways adopted in the West, where some Middle Eastern names still survive. One such garment was the *caftan*, a full-length, long-sleeved, ample robe, with buttons down the front. It was originally worn by both men and women, later, in some regions, by women only. This name, and the garment it designates, became known in the West at an early date and is already attested in English in the 16th century. Another garment of Middle Eastern origin is the pajama, a word of Persian origin literally meaning "leg-garment." The word, along with the garment that it designates, traveled from Persia to India, where it was picked up first by the Portuguese and then by the English, and brought to Europe. Originally, it denoted loose trousers, normally made of cotton or silk, and tied round the waist. Later, it was extended to include a kind of jacket and restricted to denote garments used for sleep.

In countries of warm climate, like Arabia and Egypt, men wore— and to a large extent, still wear —loose white garments that hang from the shoulder and cover the whole body down to the ankles; sometimes they are caught at the waist by some sort of sash or bandolier. One such is the *galabiyya*, still commonly worn in Egypt. Others include the *thob* and the *dishdasha*, worn in much of Arabia.

Two Iranians wearing turbans and abayas in the holy city of Qum.
(FotoSearch)

Trousers were not part of the original dress of the Arabs, and they remain alien in Arabia to the present day. They were, however, known from very early times and were apparently introduced from Persia. There are indeed some who think that trousers were a Persian invention. They became known to the Arabs from the time of the Arab conquest of Persia in the 7th century, if not earlier. Tradition ascribes them to an even remoter past. According to a hadith, "The first to wear trousers was the prophet Abraham. Therefore, he will be the first to be clothed on the Day of Judgment." According to another hadith, Moses was wearing woolen trousers on the day when God spoke to him. The general view is that the wearing of trousers by men is permitted, but not recommended. It is, for example, forbidden for pilgrims and disapproved even for prayer. In contrast, the wearing of trousers by women is strongly recommended. Early hadiths quote the Prophet as saying that it is good for women to wear trousers, both for their protection and for decency.

Despite this disapproval, trousers were sometimes worn by men, especially by soldiers. They also figure in various contexts as a kind of garment of honor. In general, however, they were more used by women than by men. Trousers of the familiar Western kind came to the Middle East as part of the process of Westernization. The adoption of Western-style dress began in the early 19th century and was for a long time confined to those in government service—notably the military, the bureaucracy, and others in direct contact with Westerners. Until the 20th century, those affected remained a relatively small minority and even these for the most part combined a Western suit with a more traditional headgear, such as a fez. Among women, the adoption of Western dress was more recent, much more limited, and was strongly resisted. The adoption of modern dress by women, though lagging behind that of men, nevertheless went quite far among the middle and upper classes in the cities and began to affect even the countryside. One of the most noticeable consequences of the Islamic revival has been a reversal of this trend and a return, by women though much less by men, to traditional attire, at least out of doors. Sometimes this represented a kind of compromise as, for example, in the popularity among Egyptian women students of the trouser suit, which enables them to combine Western elegance with Muslim decency. This did not, however, satisfy the Islamic militants, who demanded, and often obtained, a return to more traditional and more effective forms of bodily concealment.

The concept of clothing as badges of identity has by no means entirely disappeared. In the Islamic republic of Iran, for example, it is by now customary for men, particularly when traveling abroad, to wear Western-style shirts, jackets, and trousers. But they do not wear neckties, since the necktie, perhaps because of its vaguely cruciform shape, is seen as a Christian emblem.

Headgear has always had a special importance. Of the many different forms that have been worn in the Muslim world, a few survive, some of them vigorously, to the present day. Notable among these is the kafiyya, variously transcribed. The name is said to come from Kufa, the town in Iraq where it was first manufactured. This is a square piece of cloth, folded diagonally into a triangle and worn as a head covering. It is kept in place by a black-corded headband, known as *'iqal*, and traditionally made of camel's hair. The kafiyya is still universally worn in Saudi Arabia and is extensively used in many other places, notably among Palestinians and Jordanians. The pattern and coloring of the kafiyya often have a symbolic quality, indicating tribal or other affiliations. A well-known example of the effective use of the kafiyya in this way was provided by the late Palestinian leader Yasir Arafat. Another widely worn covering is the *burnus*, a kind of hooded cloak, usually made of wool.

Two Arabs in kafiyyas (head coverings) with iqals (black headbands) wearing dishdashas (robes).
(Getty Images)

The form of head covering most traditionally associated with Islam, by both Muslims and others, is the turban, the distinctive headdress worn by Muslim males since very early times. The name is first attested in English in the 16th century, a little earlier in French and German and, in the form *turbante*, in Italian and Spanish. It was already known to Shakespeare; in a famous passage, Othello speaks of his encounter with "a malignant and a turban'd Turk...."

The word would appear to be derived from *tulband*, the Turkish pronunciation of the Persian *dulband*, a common name in Persian and Turkish, although not in Arabic, for this form of headgear. Another word from the same source is "tulip," sometimes called "tulipan," a flower introduced to Europe from the Middle East in the 16th century, and so named because of its Middle Eastern origin and its perceived resemblance to a turban. In Arabic, both classical and modern, the common term for this form of headgear is not turban but *'imama*.

Turban-like forms of headgear are depicted in ancient Assyrian and Egyptian monuments, and a kind of turban seems to have been the normal headgear worn by bedouin in pre-Islamic Arabia. It came to be regarded as the distinguishing emblem of the Arabs, marking them off from the non-Arabs. After the advent of Islam, it acquired a new significance, distinguishing the Muslims from the unbelievers. Many sayings attributed by tradition to the Prophet stress the importance of the turban as an emblem of Islam. In medieval times, it became the custom for the caliphs and sometimes for other high dignitaries to wear large and elaborate turbans, adorned with gold and silver threads and sometimes with jewels. These formed the equivalent of the crowns worn by European monarchs.

Even among lesser mortals, there were different ways of wrapping and wearing turbans. Among other forms of head covering, we may note the cloth and crocheted caps worn by men and, of course, the head scarves and veils worn by women.

The emblematic significance of headgear is a recurring theme throughout Islamic history. From time to time, we find orders prescribing or prohibiting various types and colors of head covering, for various categories of people. There were different head coverings for Christians and for Jews, and also, by Ottoman times, different forms of headdress for different orders of society. In traditional Ottoman usage, dress, and most important, headgear, were the outward and distinguishing signs of group identity. "The turban," says an old tradition, "is the barrier separating belief and unbelief." These and other sayings of the same purport express the widespread feeling that to give up one's traditional attire and adopt that of some other social order was a kind of betrayal, a sort of treason or apostasy. This idea is an old one in the Middle East and can be traced back to Biblical times. "In the day of the Lord's sacrifice," says the prophet Zephaniah, God will punish "all such as are clothed with strange apparel" (Bible 1:8). Several traditions ascribed to the Prophet urge Muslims not to dress like infidels "lest you become like them." Non-Muslims were forbidden to dress themselves in Muslim style; Muslims would, of course, not dream of adopting Christian or Jewish dress. The hat, in Turkish, *shapka*, was regarded as the very badge and symbol of the unbeliever and the expression *shapka giymek*, to put on a hat, meant to abandon Islam and become a Christian. The English word "turncoat" conveys a similar notion. Among the Muslims themselves, each profession, each social order, had its own special type of headgear. Janissaries and other sections of the military, the ulema, the doctors of the holy law, the various orders of dervishes, the different branches of the civil service—each had their own distinctive headgear, which proclaimed their status when they were alive and was carved in stone over their graves when they died, to assert it for eternity. Among Muslims as among Jews, a covered head is a sign of respect toward both God and man.

During the 19th century, as part of the process of modernization, European dress was introduced, at first only for males in government service, and then more broadly among males in the urban upper and middle class. But while adopting such Western garments as military tunics, civilian jackets, and trousers for both, they avoided Western hats or caps, disfigured by a brim or a peak that would impede Muslim worship, and instead, devised new forms of headgear, no longer turbans, but still distinctively different from anything Western. The most widely used of these was a red cap resembling a flowerpot, named after the city of Fez in Morocco where it was first manufactured. It was introduced into Turkey in the early 19th century, at first for the military and civil servants of the state, and then more generally among the urban population. The turban was in time restricted to religious personages. The fez, by now seen as demonstratively non-Western, was abolished and outlawed in Turkey in 1928, but survived for some time longer in the ex-Ottoman Arab provinces, where it was known as *tarbush*.

Another item regarded as distinctively Arab and, since the time of the Prophet, Muslim, was the sandal. As late as the 18th and 19th centuries, special significance was attached to the wearing of sandals and of boots, the former by the believers, the latter by a variety of infidels.

A memoir by a princess in the Ottoman Imperial Palace in Istanbul describes the impact of European fashion on the ladies of the harem, in the 19th and early 20th centuries:

> "The...Imperial Princesses wore European style of dress of the height of fashion of that period. Formerly the Imperial Harem had worn Oriental dress; that is to say, heavily embroidered wide trousers, called shalwahs, and a bolero, with a transparent or highly decorated blouse with long sleeves—a jeweled cap which was sometimes ornamented with gold and silver coins on their heads—their hair done in long plaits, woven with jewels. During the reign of Sultan Abdul Aziz, when the Empress Eugenie came on a visit to Stanboul, she caused a revolution in Harem fashions. She was then in the heyday of her beauty, and the Sultan admired her openly, fêted her, and gave her magnificent jewels. The women of the Harem naturally became jealous, startled by the open admiration shown by their Lord and Padishah for this giaour [infidel]—this daughter of a race whose women had no shame and went unveiled in the presence of all men!

Little by little, European styles of dressing, of arranging the hair, crept into the Palace—perhaps they thought that which the Sultan had admired on a giaour he would like even more on them. By 1870 the old fashions had been forgotten; the skirt had replaced the shalwah (the traditional baggy trousers), and the Princess and the great ladies of rank dressed themselves with the greatest elegance and taste in the latest of European fashions of the moment."

—H.R.H. Princess Musbah Haidar, *Arabesque, Revised edition,* London *(1968), pp. 56-57.*

CHAPTER 13

Language and Writing

At the time of the Prophet's birth and mission, the Arabic language was more or less confined to Arabia, a land of deserts, sprinkled with oases. Surrounding it on land on every side were the two rival empires of Persia and Byzantium. The countries of what now make up the Arab world were divided between the two of them—Iraq under Persian rule, Syria, Palestine, and North Africa part of the Byzantine Empire. They spoke a variety of different languages and were for the most part Christians, with some Jewish minorities. Their Arabization and Islamization took place with the vast expansion of Islam in the decades and centuries following the death of the Prophet in 632 CE. The Aramaic language, once dominant in the Fertile Crescent, survives in only a few remote villages and in the rituals of the Eastern churches. Coptic, the language of Christian Egypt before the Arab conquest, has been entirely replaced by Arabic except in the church liturgy. Some earlier languages have survived, notably Kurdish in Southwest Asia and Berber in North Africa, but Arabic, in one form or another, has in effect become the language of everyday speech as well as of government, commerce, and culture in what has come to be known as "the Arab world."

For a long time, Arabic speakers constituted the majority of Muslims, and the Koran indeed observes in several places that God had now sent them a final revelation in Arabic. With the rapid expansion of Islam, by conquest and still more by conversion, and, especially with the Islamization of large parts of South and Southeast Asia, native Arabic speakers have become a minority among the followers of the faith which they founded. But Arabic remains of central importance for Muslims everywhere, whatever their native language. And in all the multiple languages of the Muslim world, whatever their origins, there is a vast vocabulary of loan-words derived from Arabic.

Arabic was not only revered as the holy language—the language of prayer and scripture and, therefore, of God and of heaven; it was also greatly admired, understandably, for its richness and depth. This is well expressed in a striking passage in a 10th century Arabic encyclopedic work, probably written in Iraq: "The perfect language is the language of the Arabs and the perfection of eloquence is the speech of the Arabs, all others being deficient. The Arabic language among languages is like the human form among beasts. Just as humanity emerged as the final form among the animals, so is the Arabic language the final perfection of human language and of the art of writing, after which there is no more." This passage, incidentally, suggests an interesting early prefigurement of the Darwinian theory of evolution.

In the Middle East, script and scripture have always been closely connected and, in the past, people of different religious communities, while sharing a common spoken language, preferred to write that language in the script of their holy books. Jews normally spoke the language of the country but wrote their various spoken languages in the Hebrew script of the Old Testament. Christians, especially in the Arabic-speaking countries, for a long time wrote Arabic in the Syriac script, following the version of the Bible which is the sacred book in some of the eastern churches. For Muslims, of course, Arabic, the language of the Koran, was the holy language, and the script in which it was written was the holy script. Just as Arabic speakers of different religions wrote the same language in different scripts, so people of different languages but the same religion, Islam, wrote these different languages in the same Arabic script.

As Islam spread east and west from Arabia, and more and more peoples were converted to the faith, new Islamic languages evolved. These were all written in the Arabic script, sometimes with the invention of additional letters to represent sounds that did not exist in Arabic. These languages also usually adopted a very considerable Arabic vocabulary, covering the whole range of religious and many associated cultural matters. The Arabic elements in Persian, Turkish, and so on, thus correspond more or less to the Latin and other non-Anglo Saxon elements in English, and result from a similar sequence of events: conquest, conversion, and cultural transformation.

Persian

After Arabic, the first major language to be Islamized and in a sense Arabized in this way was Persian, already at that time a language of venerable antiquity, and the medium of a rich and diverse civilization. The name "Persian" is derived from the province of Pars on the eastern shore of the Persian Gulf. The language of that province was called Parsi, that is, Persian. Since the sound "P" is missing in the Arabic language and therefore in the Arabic script, in Arabic usage the province and the language came to be known as Fars and Farsi. In Greco-Roman and then more generally in Western usage, the name Pars (Persia) came to be applied to the whole country. Its inhabitants, however, have usually preferred to call it Iran and, in modern times, have insisted that others also do so. The term Iranian, related to Aryan, designates a group of cognate languages, which besides Persian includes Kurdish, Tajik, and some of the languages of Afghanistan.

After the Arab conquest of Iran in the 7th century CE, the majority of Persians came to adopt the Islamic faith, and with it, the Islamic script and the Islamized version of their own language. As happened almost everywhere else in the Middle East, the old languages and scripts were forgotten, and the surviving inscriptions and other literature remained unknown and unread, except among the small and dwindling minorities who still adhered to the old religion, until they were discovered and deciphered by modern scholarship.

The third major Islamic language in the Middle East was Turkish, brought to the region by a series of migrations and invasions. Like the Persians, the Turks abandoned their earlier cults and scripts, and embraced Islam and the Arabic script. Islamic Turkish, like Islamic

Persian, was written in the Arabic script, with a very considerable vocabulary of loan words from Arabic and also from Persian.

From the Middle East, the spread of Islam, by conquest and conversion, brought the Arabic script to many new regions and languages—in the east, to south and southeast Asia, in the west, to sub-Saharan Africa and, for a while, to parts of Europe. In south Asia, the Urdu language of Pakistan and of many Muslims in India resulted from the impact of Arabic and more especially of Islamic Persian on the indigenous Indian languages. The word "Urdu" is of Turkic origin, related to our word "horde."

The Arabic script was thus a major binding force in both religion and culture, linking Muslims everywhere to each other and to the shared past of their faith. It also had a profound religious significance. Muslim worship, unlike that of many, indeed most other religions, makes no use of statuary or pictures. These are regarded as idolatrous and are accordingly banned. In mosques, there are no statues, no pictures on the wall. Nor are there any musical instruments, since these too are seen as part of idolatrous worship. What we see instead is writing— written or engraved texts in the Arabic script, mostly but not exclusively from the Koran. In writing these texts, the Muslims developed a marvelously subtle and intricate art of calligraphy, which has no equivalent anywhere in the Western world (see pp. 49-50).

All this made the shock so much greater when Kemal Atatürk (died 1938), the first President of the Turkish Republic, decided to abolish the use of the Arabic script, except in purely religious contexts, and to replace it with a modified Latin alphabet, which from then onward became the official script of the Turkish language.

He was not alone in this. In the Soviet Union, which had inherited the conquered Muslims, mostly Turkish peoples, of the Russian empire, a similar reform was accomplished. The Arabic script, in which the Muslim languages of central Asia and trans-Caucasia had previously been written, was abolished, and replaced by various versions of the Russian cyrillic script, modified to their different phonetic needs.

This continued until the breakup of the Soviet Union and the resulting change in the status of these Muslim regions and republics. Six of them, Azerbaijan, Uzbekistan, Kazakstan, Turkmenistan, Tajikistan, and Kyrgyzstan, are now sovereign and independent republics. Other Muslim peoples, notably the Chechens, remained part of the Russian Federal Republic. The Tajik language is of the Iranian family; the others are of the same language family as Turkish. This group of countries is often referred to nowadays as "the Stans." The ending "stan," of Persian origin, is often added to the name of an ethnic group to indicate the place or country where that group lives. Examples from within the region are Kurdistan and Turkistan and, from outside the region, Hindustan (India) and Inglistan, the common term for England in Persian and in Ottoman diplomatic usage.

Since the former Soviet territories became independent, there has been an ongoing debate between three different approaches to the problem of writing. Some prefer to retain the cyrillic script which they have used since the establishment of Soviet rule. Some wish to return to the Islamic, Arabic script used by their ancestors before the Russian conquest. Some wish to adopt, in a suitably modified form, the Latin script in use in the Turkish Republic. All these may be found in the "stans."

Among Muslim communities elsewhere in the world, the choice of script usually goes one of three ways: the Arabic script, the script used by the majority population, or the Latin alphabet. The most notable use of the Latin alphabet, outside Turkey, is among the vast Muslim populations of the former British and Dutch possessions in Southeast Asia, in the countries now known as Malaysia and Indonesia. In these, while previous scripts survive at various levels, the official languages are written in the Latin scripts bequeathed to them by their former imperial masters. The Persians, the Turks, and after them, various other peoples in Asia and Africa, preserved their old languages in an Islamized and Arabized form.

The situation in the countries that are now known as the Arab world, extending from Iraq in the east to Morocco in the west, was somewhat different. In these, the ancient languages were, for the most part, replaced by Arabic. In some areas, as for example among the Kurds in the east and the Berbers in the west, the old languages survived, though—because of the lack on one hand of political independence and on the other of a generally accepted common written language—with limited cultural impact. For the most part, Arabic has become the language of everyday communication at all levels—in government, commerce, education, culture, the media, and conversation.

But this, in turn, created a problem. Because of its sanctity, Arabic changed very little through the centuries. There were, of course, changes in language and usage to take account of a changing world, but nothing comparable to the process by which Latin in Europe evolved into French, Spanish, Italian, and Portuguese. In the Arab world, there was a similar development in the spoken language, and variants of spoken Arabic appear in North Africa, Egypt, Syria, and Iraq, differing as much from each other and from the classical language as do the Romance languages of Europe differ from each other and from Latin. But the difference is that, unlike the Europeans, the Arabs have never formally adopted these variants as national languages. They are seen simply as dialects, while everything that requires writing—a rapidly widening range in the modern world—is still conducted, as far as possible, in literary Arabic.

This obviously has both advantages and disadvantages. Its most immediate advantage is a level of intercommunication between different parts of the far-flung Arab world which Christian Europe has not had for a thousand years. The main difficulty is the practical one—to become literate means not only to learn a script, but also to learn a language. This problem, known as diglossia, the simultaneous use of two different forms of language, remains a serious educational problem in the Arab world. Modern communications, especially radio and television, may show the way to a solution. Thanks to the cinema and television, Egyptian spoken Arabic, previously confined to the Nile Valley, in now understood all over the Arab world.

In the meantime, the by now almost universal Latin script has made progress in a number of other Muslim countries, notably in southeast Asia and in sub-Saharan Africa. But among Muslims everywhere, the Arabic script—the holy script in which the holy Koran is written— remains an essential part of their religious, cultural, and even their aesthetic life.

There are many hadiths, sayings attributed to the Prophet, concerning jihad. Here are a few:

Paradise is in the shadow of swords.

Jihad is your duty under any ruler, be he devout or tyrannical.

A day and a week at warfare are better than a month of fasting and prayer.

He who dies without having taken part in a campaign dies in a kind of unbelief.

God himself marvels at people who are dragged to paradise in chains [an allusion to captured and enslaved infidels who are converted to Islam].

One expedition at sea is worth ten on land, and he who is seasick in the jihad at sea is the equal of one who sheds his blood in the cause of God.

Learn to shoot straight, for the space between the mark and the archer is one of the gardens of paradise.

The nip of an ant hurts a martyr more than the cut and thrust of weapons, for these are more welcome to him than sweet cold water on a hot summer day.

There are also some traditions that lay down rules for the conduct of warfare:

Looting is no more lawful than carrion.

God has forbidden the killing of women and children.

Muslims are bound by their agreements, provided that these are lawful.

CHAPTER 14

War and Peace

Muslims, like most other people, have from time to time found it necessary—or even desirable—to wage war. Like other people again, they have tried in various ways to involve their religion in their wars and thus to obtain divine sanction, help, and even reward for their military efforts and sacrifices.

In their behavior over the centuries, Muslims, with rare exceptions, have not differed greatly from followers of other religions in their conduct of warfare. There are, however, significant and interesting differences in how they perceive the relationship between war and religion, and, perhaps more particularly, in how they themselves are perceived by others in this regard.

For some time now, two contrasting images have dominated debate in the Western world about Islamic attitudes toward war and warfare, and about the role that they have played in world history. One of them depicts the Muslims as a race of ferocious and fanatical warriors, riding out of the desert on horseback, with a sword in one hand and a Koran in the other, giving their victims a choice between the two—in other words, conversion to Islam or death. The other image depicts Islam as a religion of peace, rather like the Quakers, dedicated to peaceful and friendly cohabitation with others, in an atmosphere of mutual tolerance and respect.

Both contain elements of truth; both are wildly exaggerated. A more accurate portrayal of Islamic attitudes and practices would be, as with most other matters, somewhere between the two extremes.

The fanatical warrior offering his victims the choice of the Koran or the sword is not only untrue, it is impossible—unless we are to assume a race of left-handed swordsmen. The left hand, by Muslim tradition, is reserved for unclean purposes. No Muslim could conceivably brandish the Koran in his left hand. The alleged choice—conversion or death—is also, with rare and atypical exceptions, untrue. The Koran states explicitly: "There is no compulsion in religion" (2:256). It has been suggested that this is an expression of resignation rather than an injunction of tolerance, but it is certainly in the latter sense that the verse has been understood and applied by Muslims. At the time of the Christian reconquest in Spain and Portugal and the final defeat of the Moors in the 15th century, Muslims and also Jews in both countries were given the choice: baptism (that is, conversion), exile, or death. The Muslim conquerors, in their time of triumph, offered those of their new subjects who professed one of the revealed religions an additional choice—the status known as the *dhimma* (see pp. 56, 188).

Strictly speaking, the option of the dhimma was limited to monotheists with a divine scripture, defined as Jews, Christians, and Sabaeans (Sabi'a). Polytheists and idolaters were not offered this choice, and the best that they could hope for was enslavement. This sometimes created acute problems as the Muslims advanced into Asia and sub-Saharan Africa, where the overwhelming majority of the populations did not qualify for the dhimma. Generally speaking, however, Muslim toleration of unbelievers and misbelievers was far better than anything available in Christendom until the rise of secularism in the 17th century.

The other image, of the religion of peace, is equally misleading. While Muslim behavior compares not unfavorably with that of followers of other religions, Muslim scriptures and teachings are unequivocally different and contain nothing like the pacifist doctrines of the Gospels and of some of the Hebrew prophets. Muslims are nowhere commanded to turn the other cheek, or to love their enemies or even their neighbors, and they are not promised a time when "they shall beat their swords into plowshares...nations shall not lift up sword against nation, neither shall they learn war anymore" (Bible, Isaiah II:4). Koranic precepts and Muslim practice are much closer to the earlier books of the Old Testament and more particularly to Joshua.

Because war is permitted and in certain circumstances even required, it is regulated by holy law, which deals in considerable detail with such matters as the opening, interruption, and termination of hostilities, the conduct of warfare, the treatment of noncombatants and prisoners, permitted and forbidden weapons and tactics, etc.

According to Shari'a, Muslims may lawfully wage war against four types of enemy:

- Infidels
- Apostates
- Rebels
- Bandits

The first two—wars against non-Muslims and against renegade Muslims—qualify as jihad, with all that that designation implies. The third and fourth, against Muslims defying the authority of the Muslim state, do not qualify as jihad, and the rules of warfare are somewhat different. In principle and in theory, there was only one universal Muslim state, headed by the caliph. In practice, this ceased to be so, and in fact, the Islamic world, for most of its history, was divided into a number of states, under different dynasties of rulers, sometimes at war, sometimes at peace with each other. The use of the term "rebels" is a legal device, to legitimize both peaceful and war-like relations between Muslim rulers, in theory impossible, since in theory there is only one Muslim sovereign. Bandits were seen as criminals, and treated as such; rebels were another matter, and in dealings with them, each side in an internal conflict could view his enemy or interlocutor as a rebel. This made it possible to regulate both warlike and peaceful relations between separate Muslim states according to the rules of Islamic law. The term "rebels" denotes, in fact if not in theory, independent Muslim belligerents, entitled to be treated as such according to the laws of war. One significant difference may be noted: In a jihad, captured enemies, along with their families, could be enslaved and either used or sold. Captured rebels or bandits, being Muslims, could not.

The word *jihad* comes from an Arabic root with the basic meaning of striving or effort. In the Koran, it usually appears in the phrase "striving in the path of God."[1] In scripture, tradition, and elsewhere, the term jihad is used with two related but different meanings—moral striving and armed struggle. It is usually clear from the context which of these connotations is intended. In the early chapters of the Koran, dating from the period when the Prophet was still the leader of a minority struggling against the dominant oligarchy in Mecca, the word is often used in the moral sense. In the later chapters of the Koran, dating from the time when the Prophet was a head of state and commander of armies in Medina, it usually has a more practical, even specifically military meaning:

> Not equal are those Believers who sit (at home) and receive no hurt, and those who strive and fight in the cause of God with their goods and their persons, God hath granted a grade higher to those who strive and fight...than to those who sit (at home). And to all (in faith) hath God promised good; but those who strive and fight has he distinguished above those who sit (at home) by a special reward.[2]

The jurists of the holy law distinguish between offensive and defensive jihad. In offense, it is an obligation of the Muslim community as a whole, and may therefore be discharged by volunteers and professionals. In a defensive war, it becomes an obligation of every free, able-bodied, adult male.

In the traditional view, the world is divided into two parts: the House of Islam (*Dar al-Islam*), where Muslims rule and Muslim law is enforced, and the House of War (*Dar al-Harb*), the rest of the world where infidels still rule. According to traditional teaching, the obligation of jihad will continue until all the world either adopts Islam or

---

[1] Koran 5:35; 9:24, 41, 44, 73, 86; 25:52; 60:1, 11; 66:9.

[2] Koran 4:95; 7:72; 9:41, 81, 88; 66:9, etc.

submits to Muslim rule. This perpetual war may be interrupted by truces, which may even be of long duration, but it does not end until final victory. In fact, such "truces" do not differ greatly from the so-called "treaties of peace" that punctuated the military and diplomatic relations of rival European powers through the centuries.

In common usage, there are two different words for peace, *salam* and *sulh*, with a significant difference of meaning and usage between them.

Salam occurs frequently in the Koran and in other Islamic texts, and can be heard every day in normal conversation in virtually every Muslim language. Its normal meaning, however, is nonpolitical and has nothing to do with the contrast of peace and war. Salam means peace in this world, that is, tranquility, and in the next world, that is, salvation. It is, of course, used in the common form of greeting *Salam 'alaykum*, usually translated "Peace be with you," but literally "Peace be upon you." Traditionally, this greeting is only used when addressing fellow Muslims. For non-Muslims, other forms of greeting are prescribed and used. In traditional Muslim diplomatic usage, Salam 'alaykum is always used in communication between Muslims, even between rulers at war, as, for example, in the correspondence leading to the outbreak of war between Saudi Arabia and Yemen in 1934. The correspondence ends with a letter from King Ibn Saud to the Imam of Yemen saying, "This means war—and peace be with you." In communications with non-Muslim rulers, even with allies, another form of words was common, based on a verse in the Koran: *Al-salam 'ala man ittaba' al-huda*, meaning "Peace be upon those who follow the divine guidance," (2:49) that is, those who accept the Prophethood of Muhammad and embrace Islam. According to tradition, this was the formula used by the Prophet in the letters he sent to the current rulers of the world, the Byzantine emperor, the Persian emperor, the Negus of Ethiopia, and others, to embrace Islam or suffer the consequences. This formula was sometimes used by Muslim rulers, such as the Ottoman sultans, in addressing their non-Muslim neighbors. It was most recently used by President

Ahmadinejad of Iran in his May 2006 letter to President Bush of the United States.[3]

The word normally used for peace as opposed to war is *sulh*, which in early classical usage generally indicated a truce of limited duration. In modern Arabic usage, however, it is the term commonly used to denote major peace treaties, even where no Muslim interest is involved. At the present time, there are some changes in Arabic usage, as sulh is becoming more limited while salam is acquiring a broader and more political sense.

At certain times and places, jurists sometimes recognized an intermediate zone between the House of War and the House of Islam, which was called the House of Truce (*Dar al-Sulh*) or House of the Pact (*Dar al-'Ahd*). This was used for territories where non-Muslim rulers continued to govern their own subjects, with some measure of autonomy, but under broader Muslim suzerainty and usually subject to the payment of some kind of tribute. The classical example was the treaty made by the caliph in the year 31 of the hegira (652 CE) with the king of Nubia in Africa, in accordance with which the Nubian king continued to rule his own territory but agreed to deliver an annul levy of some hundreds of male and female slaves to the Muslims.

According to both tradition and law, Muslims who fight in the jihad are entitled to a double reward—of booty in this world, consisting of the possessions, persons, and families of their defeated enemies, and the delights of paradise in the next. The jurists distinguish explicitly between looting, which is criminal, and booty, which is a legitimate prize of war. The law books discuss at some length the definition of booty and how it is shared among the victors. Since the enslavement of free persons, Muslim or other, in the lands under Muslim rule was forbidden, and since opportunities for purchase abroad were limited,

---

[3] In the extensive correspondence of the Ottoman sultans with the various rulers of Europe, the sultans normally used a somewhat more polite formula, which might be translated: "May his (or her) end be happy." In other words, "May they finally embrace Islam before they die," a form of words which suggests courteous good will and which could be, and often was, enhanced by creative translation.

jihad became a major source for the supply of new slaves, both male and female. This was often criticized by religious authorities. From an early date, Islamic tradition makes it clear that while booty is legitimate as a reward, it must not be a motivation. Indeed, according to a widely held view, to wage jihad for reward invalidates that reward. The honorable name of jihad must not be dishonored by slave raiders and looters. Not surprisingly, in view of human nature, it was frequently used for both purposes, arousing the anger and contempt of the theologians and jurists. The holy law regulates elaborately what may be taken as booty and what may not, and how the booty is to be shared among the victors. As noted, lawful booty in a jihad includes the persons as well as the possessions and families of the defeated enemy. This remained common practice in the successive phases of the wars of expansion.

Because jihad is a religious obligation, it is elaborately regulated by Shari'a. Muslim fighters are commanded not to kill women, children, or the aged unless they attack first; not to torture or otherwise ill-treat prisoners; to give fair warning of the opening of hostilities or their resumption after a truce; and to honor agreements. In the medieval juristic literature, there are interesting discussions about the lawfulness of missiles, such as mangonels and catapults, and of chemical warfare, in the form of poison-tipped arrows and poisoning enemy water supplies. Some jurists permit, some restrict, and some disapprove of the use of these weapons.

At no time did the classical jurists offer any approval or legitimacy to what we nowadays call terrorism. Nor indeed is there any evidence of the use of terrorism as it is practiced nowadays.

Armed rebellion against authority is another matter, and in certain strictly defined circumstances, it is permitted, even encouraged. The Muslim political tradition is, in general, authoritarian, and Muslims are instructed to obey legitimate authority however strange the form in which it may appear. But there are limits to submission. Two traditions in particular express a widely and deeply held Muslim view: "There is no obedience in sin" and "Do not obey a creature against his Creator."

This has usually been interpreted to mean that if the ruler or his representative issues a command which is contrary to the law of God, that is, of Islam, then the duty of obedience lapses and is replaced, not by a right of disobedience as in Western political thought, but a duty of disobedience. This gave rise to a whole series of opposition movements within Islam, some peaceful, some violent, reflecting a wide range of thought and practice. The problem appears at an early date. Of the first four caliphs who succeeded the Prophet, known in Sunni historiography as "the rightly guided caliphs," three were murdered, and their reigns ended in a civil war, the first of many.

While armed insurrection was the usual form of active opposition, it was not the only one. Another was the method that came to be known as assassination. The word "assassin," of Arabic etymology, was brought back to the West by the Crusaders, together with lurid and mostly inaccurate accounts of how the assassins operated. The first point to note is that they were not mainstream Muslims. They came from an extremist offshoot of a radical branch of the Shi'a. The assassin operated in a very different way from the modern terrorist. He set out alone on his mission. He used no weapon but the dagger, disdaining missiles, poison, or any such weapons of mass or random destruction as existed at that time. It was with a dagger that he came right up to his target, a carefully chosen individual. The daggers of the assassins were directed against kings, princes, and other rulers, and sometimes against religious dignitaries, seen by them as representing the forces of evil within the Islamic community.

The assassin did not die by his own hand. The Islamic tradition is unequivocally against suicide. The early texts are quite explicit, including sayings attributed to the Prophet himself. Suicide is a major sin, and even if one has lived a life of unremitting virtue, by committing suicide, he forfeits paradise and sentences himself to hell, where his eternal punishment will take the form of the unending repetition of the act of suicide. There is even a *hadith qudsi,* a special kind of hadith in which the Prophet quotes God directly, to this effect. According to this text, a good Muslim was mortally wounded and lay dying on the battlefield of jihad. In order to shorten his pain, he stabbed himself with his own dagger, and God said: "My servant has preempted me. He shall not enter paradise."

This raised an interesting question, debated by the jurists. If a fighter in the jihad throws him against the ranks of the enemy knowing that this will result in his certain death, does this constitute suicide or not—will he go to hell or to heaven? The most usual answer was that he would go to heaven provided he did not die by his own hand, in which case he would go to eternal damnation.

Until comparatively recently, this was the general position of Muslim theologians and jurists. Then, a new line of interpretation was developed, according to which even if he dies by his own hand and takes a sufficient number of the enemy with him, then this is an act of true jihad, and he will be appropriately rewarded. The emergence of the by now widespread terrorism practice of suicide bombing (see *shahid*, p. 214) is a development of the 20th century. It has no antecedents in Islamic history, and no justification in terms of Islamic theology, law, or tradition. It is a pity that those who practice this form of terrorism are not better acquainted with their own religion, and with the culture that grew up under the auspices of that religion.

CHAPTER 15

Radical Islam

In earlier times, the religious definition of Islam was clear and simple, and Muslims did not go through the agonizing struggles of the early Christians to define and agree on formulations of the finer points of doctrine and belief. For Muslims, the task of definition was much easier and was classically formulated by an early authority: "All those are Muslims who testify that God is one and Muhammad is his Prophet, and who pray towards Mecca."

Later, of course, theologians and jurists sought to refine the creed and interpret the law, and in doing so, to specify other obligations, but all agreed on this basic minimum. Islam, far more than Christianity, allowed a considerable diversity of both belief and practice within the community. But certain limits had to be observed, and these have of course changed in a changing world. In earlier times, it was primarily the polytheist and the idolater who were excluded; in modern times, the atheist and the agnostic.

The ban on idolatry, at least in the literal and traditional meaning of that term, remains valid, but there are few idolaters in that sense at the present time who could threaten Islam or tempt Muslims. Atheism and agnosticism are another matter, and at least since the 19th century, these have been perceived as a threat. But even here, there was, in most Islamic lands, a large measure of tolerance. In general, as long as those who strayed in that direction observed the proprieties and refrained from any public challenge to basic Muslim beliefs, they were accepted as remaining in the House of Islam. They become dangerous, in the eyes of both conservative and radical Muslims, when their deviance assumes the form of what in Christendom is known as secularism—requiring the disestablishment of Islam as state religion, with the consequent abrogation of the holy law and its replacement by secular codes. Belief is a private matter and is not pursued; but an attack on the holy law threatens the very foundations of the Islamic polity and the Islamic society.

In the course of the late 19th and 20th centuries, secularism, in the guise of modernization, became a serious factor in many Muslim countries, and Muslim peoples, especially in the Middle East, tried in various ways to adopt and adapt such European ideologies as nationalism, socialism, and what might not unfairly be called national socialism. In religious circles, Western secular influence, even more than Western imperial expansion, was increasingly seen as a mortal threat to Islam. From time to time in different parts of the Islamic world, religious teachers and leaders appeared who tried to purify Islam from what they saw as infidel accretion or dilution. Some of these movements have become extraordinarily active and powerful in our time and are indeed the driving force in what is increasingly becoming a global struggle.

It is difficult adequately and accurately to define these Islamic movements in a language that for many centuries has been fashioned by Christian practice and usage. Some of them have been described, by outside rather than by Muslim observers, as "reformists." But in their own perception, their aim was not to reform, in the sense of modernizing, their faith, but rather to restore it to its pristine purity. There have been many such movements in the course of Islamic history and over the vast extent of the Muslim world, differing considerably in their doctrines, their methods, and the degree of success that they achieved. Some were gradualists, some radical; some peaceful, some violent. Of the latter, some were defeated and crushed; some were victorious, and were able to seize power and thus to confront, in time, the same challenges and the same problems as the rulers whom they had overthrown.

Such movements tend to grow in strength in times of trouble—of military or political defeat, of economic distress, of social strain, of national or communal humiliation. At such times there is greater plausibility in the argument that the Islamic world has taken a wrong turn; that its rulers have betrayed the true principles of the faith, and while maintaining a pretense of Islam, have adopted foreign and infidel ideas, laws, and customs. For this, they are being justly punished, and the only solution is a return to an authentically Islamic way of life.

In modern times, the first major movement of this kind was Wahhabism. Born in a remote area of desert Arabia in the late 18th century, it finally achieved power with the creation of the Saudi monarchy in Arabia in the 1920s (see pp. 212-213). The founder was Muhammad ibn Abd al-Wahhab (1703-1792), a theologian of the Hanbali school of Sunni Islam, who lived and died in Najd, now part of Saudi Arabia. The term Wahhabi or Wahhabism is applied to his followers and his teachings by opponents and outsiders, not by its followers, who prefer to call themselves *muwahhidun*, that is, pure monotheists or, simply, good Muslims. The movement arose during a period when Christian Europe was advancing against Islam in both the East and the West.

Wahhabism is a reaction not so much against the West as against the Westernizers—against those Muslims who sought to meet the threat of the advancing West by adopting Western ways, so as to defeat the Western enemy with his own weapons. The Wahhabis see this as a betrayal of Islam and believe that the only remedy for their problems is a return to authentic, pristine Islam. Wahhabi anger has not been limited to the Westernizers but is sometimes also directed against Muslims who do not share their beliefs, notably the Shi'a, seen as their main rivals in challenging the existing order. In the past, Muslims of different sects and schools had managed to live more or less peaceably side by side. For the Wahhabis, those who do not share their views are not Muslims but apostates.

Wahhabism had some influence in Najd and adjoining areas, and in particular was able to convert the local tribal ruling family, the house of Saud. But except for one or two brief episodes, this was a remote, tribal area of little importance, and for a long time had little or no impact on the rest of the Muslim world. Its major impact came in the mid 1920s when the house of Saud gained control of the Hijaz, containing the holy cities of Mecca and Medina, and established a new entity in the region, the Saudi Arabian kingdom. Before long, this kingdom was enriched by the discovery of oil and the immense funds which this placed at their disposal.

The Wahhabis thus enjoy several advantages, notably an unambiguous and passionately held belief, the support of the Saudi government, the immense prestige of the custodianship of the two holy cities of Mecca and Medina, and the control of the annual pilgrimage that brings millions of Muslims to a shared sacred experience every year. The new wealth from oil has enabled them to carry their doctrines all over the Muslim world, not only to Muslim countries, but also to—perhaps more especially—to Muslim communities living in non-Muslim countries, notably in Europe and America. It is very natural that Muslims living in non-Muslim countries should want to give their children some education in Islamic religion and culture. To provide this, they look to the obvious places—to evening classes, weekend classes, and holiday camps and schools. Increasingly, these are operated by Wahhabis, who teach their young disciples a Wahhabi version of Islam. In some Muslim countries where the state educational system is inadequate to address the needs of the rapidly increasing young generation, Wahhabi schools provide what is often the only education available.

Another very influential movement of Islamic revival was that known as the Salafiyya. The name derives from the Arabic term *salaf,* "those who have gone before," used to designate the pious ancestors representing the pure and original faith of Islam. The movement was first recorded in Egypt in the late 19th century, and, in a variety of forms, spread rapidly all over the Islamic world. Essentially, it was a movement of protest against the process of what some called modernization and others called the corruption and degradation of the faith by the adoption or imitation of alien, infidel ways. The Salafiyya movement shares a number of ideas with the Wahhabis.

These movements were in essence a protest against foreign-inspired reforms and reformism, and a return to what was seen as the authentic and undefiled faith of the first Muslims. The influence of the Salafiyya can be seen in the ideologies of Pan-Islam, in a series of what one might term Muslim revivalist movements, and notably, in such organizations as the Muslim Brothers (see pp. 206-207). One of the most frequently mentioned movements of this kind at the present time is Hamas, active among the Palestinians and in control of Gaza.

One of the most important Wahhabi activities has been the establishment of free madrasas, which have had a tremendous impact. In our own day, the term "madrasa" has acquired a new and very negative meaning. In classical usage, the madrasa, literally "a place of study and teaching," was the equivalent and in a sense the precursor of the European university. It was a center of study, scholarship, and enlightenment. In our own day, it is widely and often accurately understood to denote a center of extremist indoctrination. These movements also concern themselves with the struggle against Western imperialists, missionaries, orientalists, freemasons, foreign educational establishments in Muslim lands, and what they regard as dangerous movements within Islam, notably the Sufis and the Shi'a. The Salafiyya, like the Wahhabis, are overwhelmingly Sunni.

The next major movement in Islam, that of the Iranian Revolution of 1979, was Shiite. The word revolution has been much used and misused in the Middle East, to characterize almost any violent shift of power which would more accurately be described by such terms as coup d'état. But the Iranian Revolution was a genuine revolution, in the sense in which we use that word of the French Revolution of 1789 and the Russian Revolution of 1917. That is to say, it was a major change in the whole society, a great shift of power and ideas, with an immense impact on the whole world with which it shared a common universe of discourse—in this case, of course, the world of Islam.

Ayatollah Khomeini, leader of the 1979 Iranian revolution.
(Corbis/Bettmann)

The most recent of these trends, in which in different ways all its predecessors are involved, is the group of radical and often violent factions that began in the early 1990s and continue to spread. The best known of these is al-Qaida; the best known of their leaders is Osama bin Ladin. The Shi'a have their own extremist terrorist groups, notably Hizballah, literally "the Party of God," directed from Iran and most active at the present time in Syria and Lebanon. The Iranians are even reported to have links with the strongly Sunni Hamas organization in Gaza.

≈

There has been some disagreement in finding an appropriate name in Western parlance for these movements. For those who follow and embrace them, there is no problem—they represent true Islam, authentic Islam trying to reassert itself, to purify the faith from all the infidel and alien accretions that have defiled it in modern times. For non-Muslims, as well as for the majority of Muslims who do not embrace these movements, finding a name for them is more difficult.

Osama bin Ladin.
(AP Wide World Photos)

A term widely used to designate these movements, especially in the English-speaking countries, is "Islamic fundamentalists." But this designation is in many ways unsatisfactory and indeed misleading. Fundamentalism is not an Islamic but a Western term. Indeed, one can be more specific; it is an American Protestant word, which was first used about 1910, when certain Protestant churches in the United States published a series of pamphlets called "The Fundamentals," to indicate their dissent from the mainstream Protestant churches. There were two main points of disagreement: liberal theology and Biblical criticism, both of which they rejected and condemned. A characteristic of the fundamentalists was their insistence on the literal divinity and inerrancy of the Biblical text.

These are not the concerns of the so-called Islamic fundamentalists. Liberal theology of a kind has been an issue among Muslims in the past; it may again be an issue among Muslims in the future. But it is not an important issue at the present time, and it is not about theology that the argument is joined between "fundamentalist" and what one might call "mainstream" Muslims. As for the divinity and inerrancy of scripture, this is a basic dogma of Islam. There may be Muslims, there may even be believing Muslims, who question the literal divinity and inerrancy of the Koranic text, and there have even been some in the past who presented a different view, closer to that of Jews and Christians, on scripture. But this view has not been heard for a very long time. Some Muslims may perhaps doubt the dogma, but they do not publicly challenge or even question it. This again is not the issue which divides fundamentalists from mainstream Muslims.

The term "fundamentalist" is thus inappropriate, since it is American Protestant, and inaccurate, because it refers to doctrinal issues quite different from those which concern Muslims. It has also been criticized as being derogatory—a term which prejudges and condemns the movements and ideas which it purports to denote.

Unfortunately, the substitutes that have been proposed and sometimes used are not much better and perhaps even worse. In French, the term commonly used is "integriste," but this, deriving from a difference of opinion within the Catholic Church in France, is open to the same objections as fundamentalist. Laterally, the practice has arisen of simply referring to these groups and ideas as "Islamism" and to those who hold them as "Islamists." The problem with this term is that it conveys the impression that these movements—in their beliefs and behavior—are the mainstream of Islam and represent a characteristic expression of Islamic civilization. For precisely this reason, the followers of these movements welcome and indeed insist on this term. For the same reason, other Muslims reject it, and, for want of anything better, the term fundamentalist is now appearing even in Islamic languages, in literal translations of the word into Arabic, Persian, Turkish, and no doubt other languages used by Muslims and in Muslim countries. By now, the word fundamentalist is more widely used of the Islamic than of the American Protestant type, and the danger of misunderstanding is therefore diminishing.

Another term that is sometimes used, "Islamofascism," is very naturally resented by Muslims in general, as combining in a single word the name of their faith with that of the most universally execrated of modern movements. For the same reason, this term is seen by others as accurately defining these movements and indicating their place in true Islam.

Today, when Islamic radical movements in their various forms attract so much attention, two important facts need to be remembered: first, that most Muslims are not fundamentalists; and second, that most fundamentalists are not terrorists. Each of these when stated is self-evident, but both need to be restated because they are often forgotten or even denied. Fundamentalists have an obvious interest in denying or obscuring the first statement. Terrorists have a similar interest in denying or obscuring the second. Both groups are abetted—no doubt unintentionally—by the media, which naturally and inevitably tell us little or nothing about the vast mass of ordinary, decent people going peacefully about their business, whether in Cairo or Baghdad or Tehran or New Jersey. The distinctions between Islam and fundamentalism, and between fundamentalism and terrorism, are also obscured by the unwillingness of some Muslim communal leaders and religious dignitaries to condemn terrorist acts unequivocally. This unwillingness, and the popular mood to which it panders, have done and are doing great harm to the image of Islam among non-Muslim people.

A good example was the murder, committed by religious fanatics, of Farag Foda, a well-known Egyptian secularist writer, in June 1992. Not only did religious dignitaries fail to condemn this act of murder; one of them even argued that because a secularist is, in effect, an apostate, and because the penalty for apostasy is death, Foda was justly executed— though, he added, it would have been preferable if he had been tried and sentenced by a court before his execution. When high dignitaries of the religious establishment respond to murder in this way, one can hardly expect radical leaders and their followers to be more fastidious.

Conclusion

ISLAMIC HUMOR

Hospitality occupies an important place in the traditional code of values, and there are many narratives illustrating the duties of a host and the privileges of a guest. Here is an example:

A man was charged and found guilty of a capital crime and was sentenced by the governor to death by public execution. When all the arrangements were ready, the governor asked the condemned man if he had any last wish.

"Yes," he said, "it is a hot day, and you would not want to send a thirsty man to his death."

"Bring him water," said the governor. Water was brought and the man drank it. And the governor said, "Now let us proceed with the execution."

"What?" said the condemned man. "Would you execute your guest?"

The governor saw his point and ordered his release.

Within living memory, civilization has faced two deadly enemies, both of them powerful and determined, seeking to destroy and replace the existing order. They were at times able to command extensive and enthusiastic support, not only among their own people, but even at times in our own homelands. For these, the term "fifth column," first used during the Spanish Civil War to describe General Franco's supporters in republican territory, is not inappropriate. The first was Nazism, embodied in the Third Reich and the Axis; the second Bolshevism, embodied in the Soviet Union and its various puppets. After long and bitter struggles, both were finally defeated and destroyed—the one in a shooting war, the other in what came to be known as a "Cold War."

Today there is growing awareness that we are confronting a third such threat, similar in some respects, strikingly different in others. It is being variously named and defined—sometimes, by the politically correct, simply as terrorism without specification; sometimes, most alarmingly, simply as Islam. The term Islamofascism is naturally offensive to Muslims, both those who support and those who reject this version of their religion, but it has the merit of linking this movement with its two predecessors.

In trying to identify and define this third threat, it may be useful to look back for a moment at those predecessors. Germany is a great nation which has made an enormous contribution to civilization. German patriotism is a natural, legitimate expression of the pride and loyalty inspired in Germans by their country. Nazism is a monstrous perversion of German patriotism, and it was that which the world had to confront and defeat.

The desire for social betterment, for social justice, is also a natural, acceptable human aspiration, and that too underwent a monstrous perversion into what came to be known as Bolshevism. Both Nazism and Bolshevism were a curse to their own peoples, as well as a threat to the world, and for those peoples, defeat was liberation.

Today we face a third such totalitarian perversion—this time, not of a country, nor of an ideology, but of a religion, Islam. The leaders and thinkers of this new totalitarian perversion enjoy several advantages—a more sophisticated modern technology, both for destruction and for communication; a home society with a sense and knowledge of history, and therefore an awareness of defeat and humiliation without parallel in the past; and, thanks to changes brought about by migration and demography, a potential fifth column beyond the wildest dreams of their predecessors. Their work is facilitated and even helped by the widespread mood of guilt and self-denigration in the West, often expressed in the form of multiculturalism and political correctness. The immediate target of their attack is the Western world, previously known as Christendom. If and when they dispose of that enemy, they will surely turn to the rest of the world, the house of unbelief and, therefore, of war.

If we are to survive this threat—and it is by no means certain that we will—it is important to understand, precisely and accurately, the source, nature, and purpose of the attack—that is to say, the very identity of the enemy that we confront.

For some, the enemy is simply Islam, and the war, a new phase in the millennial struggle between Christendom and Islam for the enlightenment—and incidentally, the domination—of the world. This is a dangerously misleading formulation. It is true, Islamofascism arose among Muslims and is led and used by Muslims, in the same way that Nazism and Bolshevism were led and used by Germans and Russians. But there was an Islam before the rise of Islamofascism, and there will no doubt be an Islam after its demise. It is important to understand this, and to realize that in a profound historical sense, many Muslims see themselves not as our enemies but as our fellow victims.

In the preceding pages, we have attempted to present a picture of Islam as it really was and is—not the demonized version shared by the terrorists and their opponents, nor the apologists' sanitized version of a religion of love and peace through the ages, but rather the historic reality: Islam as it began, grew, developed, and changed through the centuries, both in theory and in practice, in different parts of the Islamic world, from the beginning to the present day. For devout Muslims, as for believers in other faiths, their revelation is of divine origin. Those who teach and practice the faith, again as with other faiths, are human and, therefore, fallible. It is with their performance, good and bad, that we are concerned. To fight an enemy, it is necessary to understand him. In the present struggle, the task of all of us is not only to fight the enemy, but also, perhaps more especially, to rescue his first and worst victims—his own unhappy people. For that, even more so, understanding is essential.

Some Practical Matters

Transcription

The Arabic script contains 28 letters, of which all but one, known as Alif, are consonants. Alif, corresponding to the Greek "Alpha" and the Hebrew "Alef," is the first letter of the alphabet. Unlike Alpha, it is not limited to the "a" sound but may be used at the beginning of a syllable or a word which starts with a vowel not a consonant.

Alif and two other letters, *w* and *y*, are also used to indicate long vowels and compound vowels or diphthongs.

Arabic orthography indicates only three short vowels, three long vowels, and two diphthongs:

- The three short vowels are *a* as in hat, *i* as in bit, and *u* as in put. These vowels are not represented by letters of the alphabet but are indicated by small signs which are added above or below the letters. Normally, these signs are only used in sacred texts, educational texts, and poetry.
- In scholarly transcription, it is customary to use an accent to distinguish between the short vowels and the long vowels, as follows:
  ā or *â* variously pronounced as in sand, dart, and hall
  ī or *î* as "ee" in feet
  ū or *û* as "oo" in boot
- The two diphthongs are *ay*, pronounced like "i" in hide and sometimes like "a" in pale; and *aw*, like "ow" in town.

These are the formal rules of classical and modern literary Arabic orthography. Of course, like every other language, Arabic varies greatly from time to time and from place to place, in the course of more than 14 centuries of recorded use and in a range of countries extending from the Iranian border to the Atlantic Ocean. Quite apart from local dialects, even the pronunciation of classical or literary Arabic may vary considerably.

A further complication is that Arabic names, as well as being differently pronounced, have also been differently heard and transcribed by foreign visitors in various parts of the Arab world. Thus, for example, a common Arabic word for a river valley was heard and transcribed by Englishmen in the Middle East as *wadi*, by Frenchmen in North Africa as *oued*, and by Christians in medieval Spain as *guad*. *Guad* still figures in a number of place-names on the map of Spain and of Spanish-speaking America, e.g. Guadalupe, Guadalcanal, and Guadalajara.

The Arabic Article

Many Arabic place-names and personal names are preceded by the definite article *al*, usually written without a capital letter and joined to the following word by a hyphen, e.g. al-Hasan, al-ʿAlamain. The article is often heard and transcribed *el* and sometimes appears also as *il* or *ul* depending on the grammatical situation.

Certain letters at the beginning of a word assimilate the *l* of the article in pronunciation but not in spelling. Thus, al-Rahman is pronounced "ar-Rahman"; al-Nasir is pronounced "an-Nasir." This change is sometimes observed, sometimes ignored in transcription.

The Arabic script also contains certain letters representing sounds which do not exist in English or in most other Western languages. Thus for example, the Arabic letter *qaf* is a gutteral "k," pronounced further back in the throat. This is sometimes represented by the Latin letter *q*, sometimes ignored and rendered by *k*. An obvious example is the Muslim scripture, the name of which, literally transcribed, would be *Qurʾan*, but which is commonly written *Koran*. The form sometimes used, Alkoran, is simply Koran prefixed by the Arabic definite article.

Another letter which has no precise equivalent is the Arabic letter 'ayn, representing a deep gutteral sound. In scholarly transcription, this is usually represented by ', as for example in 'Alī. In nonscholarly transcription, it is usually omitted altogether.

In Persian, Turkish, and other Islamic languages, some Arabic sounds are changed, and some new letters added, to represent sounds which do not exist in Arabic. The most common examples are *p* as in put, *ch* as in church, and "zh," like the English *s* as in pleasure.

A good example of the variety and sometimes eccentricity of transcription may be seen in the name of a medieval Muslim hero. A precise transliteration of his name from Arabic would read Salāh al-Dīn. This was often heard and transcribed in the form Salaheddin, with minor variants. He is well known in Western historiography as Saladin.

Gender

Arabic has two genders, masculine and feminine. The feminine ending is *at* or simply *a*, sometimes transcribed *ah*. Neither Persian nor Turkish words vary for gender.

Plurals

The regular Arabic plural for masculine words is formed by adding *ūn* or *īn* according to case. A large proportion of Arabic words, however, have what are known as broken plurals, where the plural is indicated by a change of vowels. This is, of course, common also in English—e.g., foot, feet; mouse, mice; man, men; woman, women.

Personal Names

In the modern Western world, people's names fall into a well-recognized and generally accepted pattern. The first name is personal and is given by the parents to the newborn child. They may name the child after a forebear, some other person, or they may simply choose a name that pleases them. In British English, this first name is commonly known as the "Christian name," irrespective of the child's religion.

The last name, also called the surname, is the family name, transmitted in the male line from the father to child. In the past, it was usual for a woman, on marriage, to abandon her paternal family name and adopt that of her husband. This once universal practice is now frequently set aside by young women wishing to retain their own ancestral names.

This originally Western pattern of naming is now widespread in the world. In the Islamic lands, it is still fairly recent and is not followed everywhere. In particular, family last names or surnames in the Western sense of the word were, until modern times, almost unknown, and they are still by no means universal.

The traditional Arab-Islamic personal name was normally made up as follows:

1. **The *Ism*, the personal name**—The most popular names all over the Muslim world are still the Arab names sanctified by scripture and early Muslim history. They may be of several types, of which the following are the most common:
   a. Biblical names in their Koranic forms, such as Harun (Aaron), Ibrahim (Abraham), Sulayman (Solomon), and Isma'il (Ishmael).
   b. Other Arab names, largely pre-Islamic in origin, most of them being Arabic adjectives or nouns, e.g. Ahmad, 'Ali, Hasan, Husain, Muhammad, 'Uthman. Some of these are often used with the Arabic definite article, e.g. al-Hasan, al-Asad ("the lion").
   c. Compound names, usually consisting of 'Abd (slave) followed by Allah (God) or by one of the ninety-nine divine attributes, such as 'Abd al-'Aziz, "Slave of the Mighty"; 'Abd al-Majid, "Slave of the Glorious"; 'Abd al-Karim, "Slave of the Generous." Other compounds with Allah are also used: Ni'mat Allah, "Grace of God"; Hibat Allah, "Gift of God", etc. Among the Arabic-speaking Christians, such compounds as 'Abd al-Masih, "Slave of Christ," may also be found.

Non-Arab Muslims have also used a certain number of non-Arab names, such as Persian and Turkish names drawn from old Iranian and Turkish history and legend. In modern times, there has been a tendency among non-Arab Muslims to use names derived from an even more remote past, such as the Mongol Jengiz and the Hun Atilla. But Arab names still predominate.

2. **The *kunya***—Usually a name compounded with Abu ("father of") or Umm ("mother of"), Abu being frequently written Bou in North Africa. Thus, Abu Musa 'Ali = 'Ali, the father of Musa; Abu Ishaq Ibrahim = Ibrahim, the father of Ishaq; Umm Ahmad = the mother of Ahmad.

   The *kunya* is not necessarily real. It may be metaphorical, referring to some desired quality: for example, Abu'l-Barakat, "father of blessings," Abu'l-Fadl, "father of merit," Abu'l-Khair, "father of good." Sometimes it is a nickname, based on some personal characteristic: e.g. Abu'd-Dawaniq, "father of pennies," a name given to the 'Abbasid Caliph al-Mansur, noted for his stinginess; and Abu Naddara, "father of spectacles," the soubriquet of a well-known (bespectacled) Egyptian journalist of the 19th century. Even when followed by a name, Abu does not necessarily refer to a real person. The *kunya* may express the hope for a son and the intention of giving him a certain name. Many *kunyas* are automatically attached to certain names (*ism*) by custom, often based on Biblical or historic precedent. The names of the patriarchs provide a frequent example. Thus, a man called Ibrahim might be given the *kunya* Abu Ishaq, Ishaq might be called Abu Ya'qub or Abu Isma'il, and so on. The *kunya* always precedes the proper name.

3. **The *Nasab* or pedigree**—Naming the father and a variable list of ancestors, each name being introduced by the word *ibn*, "son of." This is also written *bin* and *ben* and is often abbreviated to *b*. The feminine is *bint*. Writers may quote as many generations as they feel to be necessary, and in extreme cases, will go all the

way back to Adam. The usual practice is to give one or two; e.g. 'Ali b. Muhammad b. Ahmad = 'Ali, son of Muhammad, son of Ahmad. It is not uncommon for an ancestor in the list to be mentioned by a name other than his *Ism*; e.g. 'Ali b. Abi Talib = 'Ali, the son of Abu Talib (the father of Talib).

In Persian, the word *ibn* is usually omitted, and replaced by the particle *i* (also written *e*); e.g. Hasan-i Sabbah = Hasan, son of Sabbah. In the Muslim lands generally at the present time, with the exception of Morocco, *ibn* is no longer used in this sense, and the name and father's name are simply juxtaposed; e.g. Ahmad 'Ali = Ahmad, son of 'Ali. The Persians, followed by the Turks, often use *zade* ("son"), added as a suffix to the father's name or title, which is placed before the *ism*; e.g. Qadizade, "son of a judge," Kemalpashazade, son of Kemal Pasha'. The Turkish word *oglu* is also used in the same way; e.g. Hasanoglu, son of Hasan. Many of these names in *zade* and *oglu* have become surnames of a sort, borne by whole families and referring to a common ancestor rather than to an immediate progenitor, such as Osmanoglu, a name borne by descendants of the Ottoman imperial house. In the same way, the Arabic *ibn* may sometimes refer to an ancestor rather than a parent and be used as a kind of surname. Such, for example, are Ibn Khaldun, Ibn Sina (the Avicenna of the schoolmen), and, of course, Ibn Saud, the dynastic name of the reigning kings of Arabia.

4. **The *Laqab***—An honorific or descriptive epithet, sometimes a nickname, often a title. In its original and simplest form, it is a nickname usually referring to a physical quality; e.g. at-Tawil, "the tall"; al-A'war, "the one-eyed"; al-Atrash, "the deaf." At a later date, Persian and Turkish *laqabs* are encountered, as well as Arabic; e.g. Jehangir, "world-seizer"; Yildirim, "thunderbolt." *Laqabs* of a different character were adopted as throne-names by reigning caliphs and sultans. *Laqabs* of honor were also given as titles to princes, statesmen, generals, and high officers of state, generally. These are usually compounds with *Din* ("faith")

or *Dawla* ("state"); e.g. Badr ad-Din, "full moon of the Faith"; Jalal ad-Din, "Majesty of the Faith"; Siraj ad-Dawla, "Lamp of the State"; Nasir ad-Dawla, "Defender of the State." Similar compounds may be formed with *Mulk*, "Kingdom," as Nizam al-Mulk, "Order of the Kingdom;" with *Islam*, as Sayf al-Islam, "Sword of Islam," etc. Many persons are known principally by their *laqabs*, e.g. Saladin = Salah ad-Din. In the course of time, many of these *laqabs* ceased to be titles borne only by ruling princes and their officers and became little more than personal names used by all and sundry.

5. **The *Nisba***—An adjective, usually derived from the place of birth, origin or residence, sometimes from the sect, tribe, or family, occasionally from a trade or profession. A man may, thus, have several *nisbas*, as al-Qurashi al-Hashimi al-Baghdadi as-Sayrafi, "of the tribe of Quraish, of the house of Hashim, of the city of Baghdad, the moneychanger." In Arabic, the *nisba* is almost always preceded by the definite article and ends in *ī*. Among the Turks, the place *-nisba*, with the ending *li* (or *lu*), is normally placed at the beginning of a name; e.g. Izmirli Ali Riza, the Smyrniot Ali Riza. The *nisba* may be arbitrarily handed down from father to son, though its original relevance is lost.

None of these components strictly speaking amounts to a surname, though in practice, the *nasab*, *laqab*, or *nisba* is sometimes so used. Its use, however, is optional and arbitrary.

In the contemporary Islamic world, the custom is to use two names, the first of which is the personal name, the second usually being the father's name. It may, however, be equally the name of the grandparent or remoter ancestor, or a second personal name adopted by choice or given in the family, at school, in the army, etc. or one of the above-mentioned categories. The use of surnames is spreading among the literate classes, and the introduction of compulsory registration in several countries will accelerate their adoption. In Turkey, the adoption of surnames was imposed by law in 1934.

In general, Muslims all over the world use the name of the Prophet, of his predecessors, and of the early heroes of Islam, with local differences, of course, of pronunciation and sometimes even of spelling. With certain exceptions, Sunni and Shi'a Muslims use the same names. The exceptions are those early figures who are seen, by the Shi'a, as usurpers and oppressors, such as Umar and Uthman. Shi'ites have a natural preference for the names of their own early heroes and martyrs, such as Ali, Hasan, and Husain. But these names are also commonly used by Sunni Muslims.

The Muslim Calendar

Muslims, like Christians, created a new calendar with a new era, beginning with the founder of their faith. Unlike the Christians, however, they did not date it from the birth of the Prophet Mohammad but from his migration from Mecca to Yathrib, later known as Medina. The Arabic name for the migration is Hijra, in English, commonly misspelled Hegira. According to traditional accounts, the Prophet left Medina on the date corresponding to 16 July 622 and arrived in Medina on 22 September of the same year. The Muslim calendar, dating from the beginning of the Arab year in which the Hijra took place, was formally promulgated by the second caliph, Umar, some 17 years later and has been universally used in the Muslim world ever since. The Hijra is seen as an epoch-making event and the dawn of a new era. Unlike Christians, Muslims did not usually reckon backward as well as forward from the beginning of their eras. There is no accepted Muslim equivalent of the Western system of dating known as BC ("Before Christ") or, more recently, BCE ("Before the Common Era"). On contrasting attitudes toward earlier history, see Chapter 7, "Some History."

From early times, this calendar posed some problems. The Muslim year is purely lunar, consisting of 12 months, each containing 29 or 30 days. The year is thus approximately 11 days shorter than the solar year. Unlike the Jews and the Christians, the Muslims did not adopt the corrective of leap years, with the result that in the course of a century, the individual months, and therefore, all the feasts and fasts of the calendar, rotate through all the solar seasons.

Muslims, like others, accepted the ancient divisions of the day into 24 hours. In traditional Muslim usage, however, the day did not begin at midnight, as in the Western world, but from sunset, as in the ancient and still current Jewish traditions. Muslims have disagreed in the past as to whether the beginning and end of the day (and therefore of feasts and fasts) should be determined by calculation or by observation.

The beginning of the 15th century of the Muslim era—that is, the first day of the first month of the year 1400, corresponded to 21 November 1979. The year 1430 of the Hijra begins on 29 December 2008 CE.

Since the Muslim lunar year does not correspond to the seasons, and since the government finances for so long depended on such seasonal matters as the harvest, it was found necessary from an early date to use other calendars for fiscal and, more generally, for bureaucratic purposes. Sometimes these were the pre-existing solar calendars, Christian and other, in the countries that embraced Islam; sometimes they were solar adaptations of the Islamic calendar. The most important of these is the Iranian solar era, introduced in 1925. The numbering is based on the Hijra, but it is calculated in solar years, using an adaptation of the old pre-Islamic Iranian month names. This era is now used in Iran for most purposes other than purely religious, for which the Hijra calendar is used, and international, for which the Common Era is used. The Iranian New Year, the first day of the first month of Farvardin, falls in the third week of March. To convert the Iranian solar year to the Common Era, add 622 to dates from 1 January to 21 March, and 621 to dates from 21 March to 31 December.

Food and Drink

Muslims, like Jews and unlike Christians, are bound by certain rules concerning food and drink, though these rules, except for the ban on wine, are much less restrictive than those of the Jews.

Food which is permitted is known as *halal*, a word used in much the same way as kosher among Jews.

The pig, in all its forms and products, is categorically forbidden; so, too, are carrion, blood, anything tainted by blood, and any meat not slaughtered according to the rules, that is, with a sharp knife in the throat.[1]

In two places in the Koran, wine is explicitly forbidden. This ban on wine was extended to apply to other intoxicants, brewed and distilled as well as fermented, as these became known and available.

Interesting new situations arose when coffee (see Chapter 10, "Islam and the Economy") and tobacco first became known in the Muslim world, the former from Africa in the 15th century and the latter from America in the 16th century. After some debate, coffee was eventually declared lawful and is so regarded all over the Muslim world. Tobacco is now seen as lawful by most Muslims, but is still banned by some, notably the Wahhabis.

At the present time, Muslims everywhere agree on three general principles:

1. No pig meat, carrion, or blood.
2. No meat of any animal, unless it has been slaughtered according to the rules laid down and with the appropriate blessing. This does not apply to fish or locusts, which may be eaten without ritual slaughter or benediction. In this, as in so many other matters, some local customs have survived into the Islamic period, and are regarded, mistakenly, as part of the holy law of Islam. These include bans on a variety of animals, birds, and other creatures.
3. No intoxicants.

---

[1] Koran 2:168, 172–173; 5:2, 4–6, 90-91; 6:118-119, 121, 145–146; 16:114–118.

Terms and Topics

Abaya: A black over-garment, either a large square of fabric draped from the shoulders or head or a long caftan. It is the traditional form of Islamic dress for women in many countries of the Arabian peninsula, and it is sometimes adopted in other parts of the Islamic world. The abaya covers the whole body except the face, feet, and hands. It can be worn with the *niqab* (see p. 207), a face veil covering all but the eyes. Some women also wear black gloves to cover their hands.

'Abd: The Arabic word for slave (see *Slavery*), sometimes also used to designate black people. At the present time, this word appears most commonly in personal names, on the pattern of 'Abd Allah (Abdullah), "the slave of God." In this, the word Allah may be replaced by any one of the ninety-nine divine names. (See also the "Personal Names" section in the Appendix, pp. 171-176.)

Aga or **Agha**: An old Turkish title derived from a word meaning elder brother. Originating in Central Asia, it spread across Iran to Turkey. In Iran and Central Asia, it has long been used and is still used to some extent as a respectful form of reference and address. It became a more formal title in the Ottoman Empire, given to a number of officers of medium and lower grade and to a few high dignitaries. The two most important of these were the Aga of the Janissaries, the Commander-in-Chief of that famous Ottoman infantry corps and at times of the whole military establishment of the Empire; and the Aga of the Girls, the title of the head of the corps of black slave eunuchs who policed and guarded the imperial harem. He was an important and powerful figure in the palace household (see *Saray*). In late Ottoman times, the title *aga* was commonly used for military officers up to the rank of lieutenant-colonel who were unable to read and write. If they overcame this disability, they were accorded the more dignified title of efendi (see pp. 190-191). Together with all other titles, *aga* was formally abolished by the Turkish Republic but survived in Turkish popular usage as a form of address or reference for the lower classes of society and more particularly for illiterates. In other parts of the Islamic world, it retains its more distinguished status.

Aga Khan: A title used by the Ismaili Imams of the Nizari line. Though the line goes back to early medieval times, this particular title dates from the 19th century and is derived from the honorific titulature of the court of the Shahs of Persia. The first holder of the title (1800-1881) moved to India in 1840. His descendants, the later holders of that title, played an important political and latterly also social role in India, in the British Empire, and more recently in the United States. (See also *Isma'ili* and *Nizari*.)

Alawi or **Alawite**: The name of a sect of the Shi'a, chiefly represented in Turkey and in Syria, where they were long known by the name Nusayri. The Alawis are regarded as deviants alike by the mainstream Shi'a, the Ismailis, and of course, most of all, the Sunnis. They nevertheless form an important population group in both countries.

Amir: Also written *emir*, an Arabic title widely used in the Arab lands and beyond as a title of sovereignty, and also, at some times and in some places, as a claim to something less than fully sovereign authority. Amir al-Mu'minin, usually translated "Commander of the Faithful," was one of the earliest titles of the caliph (see pp. 82-84); its use remained a caliphal prerogative and was interpreted as a claim to supreme Muslim political sovereignty. In medieval times, amir was used more widely by a number of regional rulers exercising effective independence under the nominal suzerainty of the caliph. In modern Saudi Arabia, it has been given to governors of provinces, some important heads of tribes, and some other dignitaries. It was used as a regnal title by the ruler of Transjordan until 1946 when it was replaced by "king." It is still used in some other Arab principalities known as "emirates." At the present day, it is most commonly used to designate members of reigning families other than the sovereign. In this sense, it is customarily translated "prince."

Arak: An alcoholic drink variously made from palm leaves, grapes, or dates, and usually flavored with aniseed. It is known in Turkish as *raki* and in Greek as *ouzo*. It is forbidden, like all alcoholic drinks, by the holy law of Islam but is very widely drunk in the Middle East.

Assassin: A name apparently derived from the Arabic *hashishiyya*, a derogatory term used in Syria to designate a certain branch of the Isma'ili (see pp. 63-64, 152) sect. The name has been variously explained. One theory is that they were called hashishiyya because they indulged in hashish. Another more plausible explanation is that their strange behavior was said to resemble that of hashish addicts.

The Western meaning of the word assassin derives not from the beliefs but from the tactics of the sect. A militant extremist group of Isma'ilis, they were radically opposed to the ruling Sunni establishment and dedicated to its overthrow. It was they who developed and utilized the tactic of murder of a targeted individual. Their victims were always persons of consequence; usually political, military, or, less frequently, religious and judicial figures. Their method was to send a killer, carefully trained, prepared and disguised, to accomplish the execution. They appear to have seen the murder as a kind of sacrament. The murderer never appears to have attacked or even endangered any person other than the intended victim. And having killed his man, he made no attempt to escape, but allowed himself to be killed by the victim's guards. Indeed, from contemporary evidence, it was considered shameful among the Assassins for an emissary to survive such a mission.

The group originated in Iran in the late 11th century and developed a tactic of seizing or building fortresses in remote mountain areas and using these as bases from which to launch their attacks. From Iran, they extended their activities to Syria, where they used similar tactics, sometimes against the Crusaders, through whom their name became known in Europe.

A few points need to be noted about the original bearers of the name assassin. The first is that they were an extremist fringe of a radical group, very far from mainstream Islam. The second is that their attacks were always carefully targeted, without what is nowadays known as collateral damage. The third is that with very few exceptions, their victims were Muslims, members of the Sunni establishment, that their purpose was to overthrow. And finally, one might add, their movement ended in total failure and insignificance. The Assassins, as a militant Islamic group, were most active in the 11th and 12th centuries and were finally crushed in the 13th. By the 14th century, the word was already in common use in Europe in a general nonspecific sense and was defined by a 14th scholar simply as "one who kills for money"—something very different from the original bearers of the name.

Ayatollah: Literally, "[miraculous] sign of God," a title used by the Shi'a in Iran and latterly also in Iraq for the highest rank in their religious hierarchy. Both the title and the hierarchy are of comparatively recent origin. An even more recent development is the title *Ayatollah-i 'Uzma*, literally the "greatest [miraculous] sign of God," commonly translated "Grand Ayatollah."

Bakhshish: Originally a Persian word meaning "a gift," it is used in all the languages of the Middle East to describe any kind of cash gratuity or inducement, from the beggar's alms and the driver's tip to the official's bribe and the Pasha's "contribution." As originally used, the term was not necessarily negative in its implications. It evoked, rather, the gift or largesse bestowed by a superior on an inferior. A good example was the series of gifts distributed by a new Ottoman sultan, celebrating his accession, to various civil and military dignitaries. In more modern times, it has sometimes acquired a connotation of corruption, though this is not the usual or normal meaning, which is simply "tip." For bribes and the like, other terms are used.

Bayram: A Turkish term corresponding to the Arabic *'Id* (see p. 197). The two major festivals of the Muslim year are known in Turkish as the greater and the lesser Bayram.

Bazaar: A word of Persian origin, also used in Turkish and other Islamic languages, to designate a marketplace. The Arabic equivalent is *suq*, sometimes transcribed *souk* and *souq*. In premodern times, the merchants and craftsmen of the marketplace, organized in guilds and corporations, played an important part and sometimes even a political role in the life of Muslim cities. They derived some strength and even independence from the fact that their leaders were not appointed from above but chosen from within the merchant community. Modernization has reduced but not eliminated that role. Bazaars are found throughout the Middle East, from small villages to large cities. The grand or covered bazaar in Istanbul has more than 5,000 merchants under its roof. The labyrinths of shops and workshops are divided into areas selling the same merchandise. Acres of carpets, brassware, waterpipes, handicrafts, silks, gold, and silver are available. Bargaining is the modus operandi (see pp. 102-104).

Bedouin: From the Arabic *Badawi*, one who dwells in the desert, *badw*. A term applied from early times to the pastoral nomads of Arabia and later of other desert areas conquered by the Arabs in the Middle East and North Africa.

Begum (also **Begam**): A feminine form of the Turkish *Bey*. It is first attested in India during the period of Mogul rule (16th–18th centuries) and was used as a title for female members of the reigning house. In the course of time, its use was extended more generally to Muslim ladies of noble or high status. By now, all married women in Muslim South Asia of what one might call the middle and upper classes are called begum. It is also used as a respectful form of address to ladies. The title is little known in Muslim lands outside the Indian subcontinent.

Bey: Originally *beg*, a Turkish title widely used in the Ottoman Empire and its successor states. It can be traced back in Turkish usage to Central Asia and may be derived from the old Iranian royal title *bag*, itself connected with the pre-Islamic Iranian name of God. The same word occurs in the place-name Baghdad, an old Iranian term literally meaning "God gave."

In the Ottoman Empire, the term *bey* denoted rank and authority, the latter, however, subordinate to some higher authority such as a pasha (see p. 209). In the modern Middle East, it has become no more than a respectful form of address or reference. A similar devaluation of titles may be seen in the German *Herr*, the French *monsieur*, the Spanish *señor*, the English sir and mister, all of which began as titles of nobility or at least gentry.

Bismillah: Literally, "in the name of God." The fuller version would be Bısmi-llahiʻr-rahmaniʻr-rahim, "In the name of God, the merciful and the compassionate": a pious invocation uttered by Muslims at the beginning of any new undertaking—new clothes, a meal, some new task, and so on. It is said that the reference to mercy is omitted when slaughtering animals or going into battle.

Bohra or **Bohora**: A branch of the Ismaʻili sect, consisting of those who remain faithful to the line of the Fatimid caliphs despite the split after the death of the Caliph al- Mustansir in 1035/36 CE and the secession of Nizar. Bohras are to be found chiefly in western India and in Yemen (see also Ismaʻilis, pp. 63-64).

Burqa (also **burka**, **bourkah**): Worn in Afghanistan and parts of Pakistan. It is a black or blue body-covering garment with veiled eyeholes.

Caliph: An Arabic word which combines the meanings of deputy and successor, adopted as title by the successors of the Prophet Muhammad in the headship of the Muslim state and community which he founded (see pp. 82-84).

Capitulations: The technical name of a system of extra-territorial privileges that until recently was one of the major grievances of Middle Eastern countries against the Western world and remains a bitter and evocative memory. The name derives from the Latin *capitula*, "chapters," a term applied in Europe to the privileges accorded by Ottoman and some other Muslim rulers to Christian states, whereby the subjects of those states were permitted to trade and, even, under certain conditions, to reside in the Muslim lands, without being subject to the disabilities normally imposed on non-Muslim subjects and residents.

The first capitulations were granted by the Ottoman Sultan to the king of France in 1535 CE. Similar grants to other European countries, and by other Muslim rulers, followed. Initially, these agreements were seen on both sides as a concession magnanimously granted by a mighty ruler to a humble petitioner. But with the change in the relative status of the Muslim and European states, the privileges claimed and exercised under the capitulations agreements greatly exceeded those originally intended, and came to include almost total exemption from local taxation and even, to a degree, from local laws. The subjects of countries with capitulatory agreements were answerable only to their own consuls, who maintained consular courts of law for the purpose. The term capitulations became associated with the other meaning of the word, "surrender," and these extra-territorial rights became a major grievance of the rising nationalist movements among Turks, Persians, and Arabs. Capitulations were formally and legally abolished in Turkey by the Treaty of Lausanne in 1923 and in Iraq by international agreement in the same year. They were abolished in Syria and Palestine by the mandatory powers, and by the government of Persia in 1928. In Egypt, where the Ottoman capitulations had been accepted by the autonomous rulers of the local dynasty, they were recognized and indeed extended during the period of British domination. After a long struggle, they were finally abolished by international agreement in 1937. No capitulations exist at the present time, though the question has arisen in the form of requests for extraterritorial privileges for foreign, nowadays usually American, troops.

Caravan: From the Persian *karvan*, meaning "a group of travelers with their riding and pack animals and their goods," organized in a convoy for protection against attack by bandits or other predators. The caravan carried supplies of food and, if necessary, water, and traveled along fixed routes, passing through oases where the caravan could be replenished. In most of the Middle East, the caravan usually consisted of camels, but horses, mules, and donkeys were also used. The shortened form "van" is used in English to denote a type of covered vehicle.

Caravanserai: From Persian, denotes a building for the accommodation of travelers, their wares, and their baggage.

Casba: Well-known to moviegoers, from an Arabic word which among other things means a "fortress" or "citadel." It is sometimes used, especially in North Africa, to denote the old part of a city.

Chador: A Persian word originally meaning "tent," denoting a garment worn by most women in Iran when they venture out in public. It is a full-length, semi-circle of fabric, open down the front, which is thrown over the head and held closed in front. A chador has no hand openings or closures but is held shut by the hands or by wrapping the ends around the waist.

Circumcision: The removal of the male foreskin. It is not mentioned in the Koran and receives limited attention in the literature of the holy law. It is, however, universally regarded by Muslims as constituting, along with abstention from pork, the immediate and practical distinction between Muslims and the rest.

The practice of circumcision varies greatly in different parts of the Muslim world. In some, it is customarily performed on the seventh day after the birth of a boy. Elsewhere, and more commonly, it is carried out at some stage in childhood, the latest being the thirteenth year. The circumcision of boys is usually an occasion for some sort of family celebration.

The circumcision, more correctly excision, of girls is not a requirement of the holy law. In many parts of the Islamic world, it is unknown. The term is used of a variety of operations which differ widely in their extent—that is, in the precise nature of what is removed from the genitalia. The excisions can range from a simple incision involving the removal of the prepuce or "hood" of the clitoris, to the traumatic operation known variously as Pharaonic or Sudanese circumcision, involving the radical excision of the external genitalia and infibulation. The distinctions are not unimportant. Each type may imply a different set of underlying reasons for the operation, ranging from a simple ritual "cleansing" to a vigorous enforcement of chastity. In other regions, it is somewhat unevenly applied. Muslim authorities are divided on this. Some do not consider it at all; others recommend but do not require it. In some parts of the present-day Islamic world where female genital mutilation is practiced, this is due to local custom rather than to Islam.

Coffee: From the Turkish *kahve*, itself from the Arabic *qahwa*. In ancient Arabia, this meant a kind of wine, but from about the 15th century, it was applied to a new drink, made from a plant imported from Ethiopia. The name may originally derive from the Kaffa region, where the plant grows wild in profusion. Coffee as a hot drink is first reported in the late 15th century in southern Arabia, where it was prized as a way of staying awake during long and otherwise exhausting Sufi (see pp. 67-69) rituals. According to the earliest mentions, it was introduced to Yemen from Ethiopia. From there, it spread rapidly up both shores of the Red Sea, to Egypt and Syria and beyond, notably to Turkey. In the early 16th century, several attempts were made by various ecclesiastical and sometimes also even state authorities to ban coffee on Islamic grounds, sometimes as a narcotic, sometimes as an intoxicant. These attempts came to nothing, and the serving and drinking of coffee became an important part of social and even public life. The first European references to this exotic Middle Eastern drink are mostly negative, but soon Europeans acquired the taste, and the habit spread very rapidly over the Western world. For a while coffee, along with sugar, was among the major exports from the Middle East to the West. Later, as Europeans learned to grow these more cheaply in their colonies, they shifted from the export to the import side of the Middle East trade balance.

Dervish: From the Persian *darvesh* meaning "poor, indigent." This is the term used to denote a member of a religious, more specifically Sufi fraternity. There are many such fraternities, each professing a version of Sufi Islam, and each with its own distinctive rites and rituals. The most famous are the Mevlevi, sometimes known as the dancing or whirling dervishes. This order, founded by the great poet Jalal al-Din Rumi (died 1273), played a role of some importance in the Ottoman Empire. Some of these orders are now strongly established in the United States. They and their version of Islam are totally rejected by the Wahhabis (see pp. 68-69, 157-158).

Dhimmi: A member of one of the tolerated non-Muslim religions, that is, those recognized by a pact, *dhimma*, in accordance with holy law. In return for the payment of certain taxes, notably the poll-tax, or *Jizya* (see pp. 56, 199), and the acceptance of certain social, fiscal, and legal disabilities, *dhimmis* were permitted the practice of their own religions and a large measure of autonomy in their own internal affairs.

The system worked well enough in the Ottoman Empire until the 19th century, when it broke down under the impact of such imported European ideas as freedom, equality, and, above all, nationality. Second-class citizenship, even with an assured and protected status, was no longer acceptable, and the various subject peoples—the Greeks, Serbs, Bulgars, Armenians, and eventually even the Jews, created their own states. This naturally aroused resentment and suspicion in Muslim ruling circles, directed immediately against those non-Muslims who remained under their rule.

At the present time, in Saudi Arabia the practice of any religion other than Islam is strictly prohibited—a ban that is rigorously enforced. In some other countries in the region, the non-Muslim communities—steadily growing smaller by emigration—have managed to achieve some sort of *modus vivendi* with the dominant order. Some of them look back with yearning on the good old days of dhimmitude. Second-class citizenship, maintained by law, guaranteed by custom and tradition, respected by both government and people, is considerably better than no citizenship and no rights at all, which is the lot of majorities and minorities alike under the rule of the tyrants that dominate so much of the Middle East at the present time (see pp. 56-58).

Dinar: The name of a gold coin, from the Latin *denarius*.

Dirham: An Arabic derivative of the Greek *drachma*, and like it, denotes both a measure of weight and a unit of currency. The dirham was, from the earliest Islamic times, the unit of silver currency. The terms dirham and dinar have been revived in some countries to designate units of currency.

Divan: At the present day, this term, in most languages, denotes a kind of long seat or couch. Of disputed etymology, the word is probably of Persian origin, but was widely used in Arabic, Turkish, and other Islamic languages, with a variety of meanings. It commonly occurs in two senses, one literary, the other bureaucratic or governmental. In the first sense, it denotes the collected works of an author, usually a poet. In the second, it was used for the written registers compiled from early Islamic times, containing administrative, financial, and other relevant information. By extension, the word *diwan* came to be used from early times not only for the registers but also, more commonly, for the offices that compiled and maintained them. This no doubt gave rise to an alternative explanation of the origin of the word—deriving it from the Persian *dev*, "a devil," and interpreting it to mean crazy or devil-possessed, in presumed reference to the sound and appearance of bureaucrats. By Ottoman times, the Imperial *divan* (*divan-i humayun*) was the name given to the Ottoman Imperial council, which in the early centuries was the central organ of the Sultan's government. We find it widely used in the related senses of a council of state, of the chamber in which the council met, and then of the long seat, against the wall, on which the councilors sat. It is in this last sense that the word has come to be used in English and other European languages, to denote an article of furniture.

Diya: An Arabic term, usually translated "blood-wit," for the compensation to be paid in case of homicide to the family of the victim. In the case of deliberate murder, they may insist on the execution of the perpetrator. Alternatively—and in cases of involuntary homicide—they may accept a specified payment in goods or money as compensation. The system, which dates back to pre-Islamic Arabia, was retained, with some modifications in Islamic law and practice. The circumstances and obligations are regulated in some detail. The highest rate of diya is payable where the victim is a male, free Muslim. The rate for a woman is half that of a man. The rate for a non-Muslim legally present in Muslim territory is variously assessed—by some authorities at the rate of one-third, others at the rate of one-half, some even at an equal rate for that of Muslims. The death of a slave must be compensated according to his replacement value.

Dragoman: From the Arabic *tarjuman*, an interpreter or translator. The word, and the profession that it denotes, can be traced back to remote antiquity in the Middle East. From the beginnings of diplomatic and commercial relations between Middle Eastern rulers and European governments, both sides employed dragomans, who often played a role of some importance in negotiations. At a time when Middle Eastern Muslims knew no European languages, and few if any European Christians knew any Arabic, Persian, or Turkish, the dragomans on both sides were mainly recruited from the local non-Muslim minorities. At first, these sometimes included Jewish refugees from Europe, who had found sanctuary in the lands of Islam. Later, they were exclusively Christian, and for the most part, recruited from the community known as Levantines (see pp. 201-203). In time, the study of Middle Eastern languages in the West and, to a very much greater extent the study of Western languages in the Middle East, made the services of the Levantines unnecessary, and both sides were able to train and appoint translators from among their own people.

Efendi: Often incorrectly written as effendi. Along with *bey*, the most widely used form of address in Turkey and the Arab east at the present time, though in recent years there has been a tendency to abandon it in favor of purer Turkish or Arab designations. The term goes back to Ottoman and before that to Byzantine origins. It derives from the ancient Greek *authentes* (later pronounced *avthendis*), "one who kills with his own hand," as distinct from one who hires or instructs others to kill, that is, one who is authentic (from the same Greek word). By a natural evolution, *authentes* acquired the secondary meaning of master or ruler. Later, efendi came to be used of various dignitaries of steadily decreasing status and eventually was little more than a polite form of reference or address. In the Turkish Republic, it has been formally abolished, along with other Ottoman ranks and titles, but remains in common use as a form of address. As a title suffixed to the name, in Turkey, it is applied more particularly to men of religion. In the Arab countries, in contrast, it came to designate the secular literate townspeople, usually dressed in European style, as contrasted with the lower classes on the one hand and the men of religion on the other.

Eid: see *'Id*.

Emir: See *Amir*.

Fallah or **Fellah**: An Arabic word, possibly of Aramaic origin, meaning "peasant." The Arabic plural is *fallahin*.

Farman: Also *ferman* and sometimes, incorrectly, *firman*: a Persian word meaning a command or order. This became the technical term for an Ottoman or Persian imperial decree, diploma, or letter-patent.

Fatwa: A ruling given in answer to a question on a point of Islamic law. It is issued by a qualified religious authority known as a *mufti* (see p. 205). The modern use of the phrase "to issue a fatwa," as an equivalent to the American "to put out a contract," is entirely without precedent in Islamic history, doctrine, or law. Its use in this sense seems to date from February 1989, when the Ayatollah Khomeini, the highest Islamic religious authority in Iran, issued a fatwa sentencing Salman Rushdie, the author of *The Satanic Verses*, and also those involved in its publication who were aware of its contents, to death (see p. 33). An even broader reinterpretation of the term occurs in the *fatwa* issued by Osama bin Ladin and his associates in February 1998, to the effect that "to kill Americans and their allies, both civil and military, is an individual duty of every Muslim who is able, in any country where this is possible...."

As indicated, the use of fatwa in this sense is an innovation of the late 20th century CE, without precedent in Islamic history, culture, or law. In the past, it was not unknown for a mufti to issue a fatwa ratifying a death sentence or a declaration of war, but this was issued by a properly constituted chief mufti; in the former case, normally after a properly conducted trial; in the latter, in response to a request from state authority.

Faqih: A specialist in *fiqh*, that is to say, Islamic jurisprudence. A *faqih* is thus a scholar of the Shariʻa, the holy law of Islam.

Fedayeen: (correctly *Fida'in*) The plural of an Arabic word meaning "one who is ready to sacrifice his life for the cause." It was used by a political, religious, terrorist group in Iran in the 1940s and 1950s. After an unsuccessful attempt on the life of the Prime Minister in 1955, the movement was suppressed and the leaders were executed. The term was revived by the militant wing of the Palestine Liberation Organization (PLO) and since the 1960s has been their common self-description.

Fez: A red cap resembling an upside-down flowerpot, named after the city in Morocco where it was first manufactured. It was introduced into Turkey in the early 19th century, while the turban was restricted to religious personages. It was abolished in Turkey in 1928, but survived for some time longer in the ex-Ottoman Arab provinces, where it was known as *tarbush*.

Frank: A term widely used in the Middle East to denote Western, that is, Catholic and Protestant, Europeans.

Genie: The common English spelling of the Arabic term *jinn*. According to Muslim belief, jinn are one of the three groups of intelligent beings created by God, the other two being angels and humans. Humans are made of dry clay, angels of light, jinn of fire (Koran 55:14-15). Like humans, they may qualify for salvation or damnation—some destined for heaven, others for hell. Jinn cannot be perceived by human senses, unless they choose to reveal themselves. This they can do in various different forms. There is an extensive and varied folklore concerning the jinn in different parts of the Islamic world. They also figure prominently in the Koran.

Hadith: A tradition concerning the actions and utterances of the prophet; after the Koran, the second most important source of law and doctrine for Muslims. According to Muslim belief, the Prophet was divinely inspired in all that he said and did. These traditions are, therefore, a valid source of doctrine and law. Unlike the Koran, they were not committed to writing during the lifetime of the Prophet but were transmitted orally. An elaborate science grew up in the early centuries of Islam, concerned with the collection, authentication, classification, and interpretation of the Hadith (see Chapter 3, "Scripture, Tradition, and Law").

Hajj: The Arabic term for the annual Muslim pilgrimage to Mecca. The same word is used in a slightly modified form as a title for those who have performed the pilgrimage (Hajj or Hajji). For Muslims, pilgrimage is one of the five basic obligations of the faith (see Chapter 2, "Pillars of the Faith").

Halal: An Arabic word meaning lawful, permitted, according to the holy law of Islam. It is thus the converse of *haram*, unlawful, forbidden. These two terms relate to the whole range of the holy law, but their most common everyday usage is in connection with food and drink. Islam, like Judaism and unlike Christianity, regulates elaborately what practicing believers are permitted or forbidden to eat and drink. Thus, for example, Islam totally prohibits intoxicants. This was usually understood to mean alcoholic drinks, but has at various times and in various places been extended to include hallucinatory drugs and even tobacco. It is, in a sense, the equivalent of the Jewish term "kosher" (see Chapter 2 and the Appendix).

ISLAMIC HUMOR

Muslims are, of course, forbidden to drink wine, but Christians and other non-Muslims were free to make, drink, and sell it. Some Christian monasteries in Middle Eastern countries became well-known for the excellent wine that they produced and served, with the result that they were sometimes used as taverns by thirsty Muslims. The story is told that the great Arabic poet Abu Nuwas (died circa 813 CE) was found one day in a monastery, with a bunch of grapes on his right, a dish of raisins on his left, and a glass of wine in his hand. Each time he took and ate a grape, then a raisin, and then drank from the glass.

"What does this mean?" he was asked.

And he replied: "I am celebrating the Father, the Son, and the Holy Spirit."

Hamula: An Arabic term for the extended family, usually applied to a group of people descended from a common ancestor. The duration of the Hamula was normally from five to seven generations. In traditional society, the Hamula usually formed a territorial group, cultivating adjoining plots of land, and cooperating economically as a matter of course and otherwise when needed. They were bound together by strong ties of loyalty, reinforced by the common practice of marrying within the Hamula, usually cousins. The Hamula formed a single group with regard to the blood-wit (see *diya*). Family honor and social obligation alike required members of the Hamula to help each other when possible, and to avenge each other when necessary. Thus, when a member of a Hamula obtained a position of power or authority, he was expected to use it to help his fellow members of the family. In terms of Western values, this might be described as nepotism. In terms of traditional values, it was the fulfillment of a social and moral obligation. Not favoring relatives, but failing to do so would be seen as an offense. The pace of modern life has often weakened and sometimes broken the Hamula, but the system, and still more its values, have by no means disappeared.

Hanafi: A follower of the school of Abu Hanifa al-Nu'man (circa 699-767) (see p. 30).

Hanbali: A follower of the school of Ahmad ibn Hanbal (780-855) (see pp. 31, 157).

Harām: Forbidden (See *Halal*).

Haram: A term meaning a sanctuary or religiously protected place. The Haramayn, the two *harams*, is a term commonly used to denote the two holy cities of Mecca and Medina.

Harem: The secluded women's quarters of an old-style Turkish or other Muslim house. The harem included wives and concubines, sometimes also female relatives, and the servants, in former times, slaves, including eunuchs, who attended and guarded them (see Chapter 11, "Women in Islam").

Hashimite: A descendent of Hashim, the great-grandfather of the Prophet. Though not necessarily directly descended from the Prophet, the Hashimites are his kinsmen, and this title was claimed by a number of dynasties, notably the Abbasid caliphs of Baghdad (750-1258 CE) and the former ruling house of the Hijaz and its descendants in Iraq and Jordan. Of these, only the last named still reigns. The official name of Jordan is the Hashimite Kingdom of Jordan (see Chapter 7, "Some History").

Heaven: See *paradise*.

Hegira: A common corruption of the Arabic *hijra*.

Hejaz (more correctly, **Hijaz**): The region in Arabia in which the holy cities of Mecca and Medina are situated. With the exception of the port city of Jedda, no non-Muslim is permitted to set foot in the Hejaz.

Hell: In Arabic, *Jahannum*: According to the Koran (11:106–107; 22:19–21; 39; 15–24; 44:43ff; 74:27–29), the damned will be in a fire which will burn their faces until their lips peel off. It will burn their skin, and each time the skin is burned, they will be given a new skin so they may continue to feel the pain. Their drink will be boiling water which shreds their guts. Boiling water will also be poured over them. They will be clad in garments of fire and beaten with iron rods. Hypocrites will be in the lowest level of hell.

Hidden Imam: See p. 63.

Hijab: The common Arabic term for the veil worn by women. In earlier times, it was also used to denote the curtain behind which caliphs and other rulers hid themselves from their households.

Hijra: Sometimes written *Hegira*, a term used for the migration of the Prophet from Mecca to Medina in the year 622 CE, according to most accounts on September 20. The Muslim calendar dates from the *Hijra*, more precisely from the beginning of the Arab year in which the Hijra took place (see the "Calendar" section in the Appendix).

Hookah (also **Narghile**): Terms derived from Arabic and Persian and adopted in India, to designate the apparatus devised for smoking through water. Besides tobacco, the mixture might include spices, molasses, etc.

Houri: From the Arabic *hur*, the plural of *hawra*, an adjective from an Arabic root with the general meaning of whiteness. The term is used to describe the beautiful virgins of paradise whose companionship is promised to the believers as part of their eternal reward. They are described in some detail in those passages of the Koran where the joys of heaven are contrasted with the torments of hell.

In the Koran (52:20; 55:56, 72–74; 56:22–23), the function of the immaculately chaste *houris*, as of the perpetually fresh youths, is to attend and serve the blessed in heaven. Some later commentaries and traditions specify the number of *houris* and assign them a more explicitly sexual role, their virginity being miraculously reconstituted after each encounter (see *Paradise*).

Ibadi: The Ibadis or Ibadiyya, a sect within Islam, and an offshoot of the Kharijites. Though distinct from both Sunnis and Shi'a, they are much closer to the former. They take their name from a 7th- to 8th- century scholar of Basra called Abdullah ibn Ibad, but the effective founder of the group was a disciple of his from Oman, which remains the main center of Ibadism to the present day (see pp. 66-67).

Iblis: The Arabic name of the devil, no doubt related to the Greek *diabolos*. He appears in Islamic literature in two roles, one of arrogant disobedience to the commands of God, the other as tempter of Adam and Eve and their descendants. In the latter role, he is also commonly called *Shaytan*, a term clearly related to Satan (see p. 211). According to some versions, he is an evil genie; more commonly, he is regarded, in the Islamic as in the Judeo-Christian tradition, as a fallen angel. He figures prominently in the Koran (see, for example, 6:1–8ff) and the last chapter (114): "I take refuge with the Lord of mankind, the King of mankind, the God of mankind, from the evil of the insidious tempter, who whispers in the hearts of mankind, from the genies and from mankind."

'Id: Sometimes spelled *Eid*. An Arabic term used to denote the two major religious festivals or holidays of the Islamic year. One of these, the 'Id al-Adha, variously known as the "Sacrificial Festival" or "Major Festival" is celebrated on the tenth day of the month of Pilgrimage, when the assembled pilgrims make sacrifices in the valley of Mina, in the hills east of Mecca. The practice of sacrificing on this day was not limited to the pilgrims, but came to be generally adopted by Sunni Muslims. The second festival, the 'Id al-Fitr, marked the end of the Fast of Ramadan. It was celebrated on the first day of the following month, Shawwal, and sometimes for days after.

Imam: An Arabic word, the everyday meaning of which is "leader in prayer." It was often extended to denote a religious leader or guide in a broader sense and even became one of the titles of the caliphs. Among the Shi'a, it was used more particularly of their own pretenders to the caliphate, and in Shi'a parlance connoted a much more extensive spiritual authority than among the Sunnis (see pp. 39-40, 62-64).

In sha' Allah: Literally, "if God pleases," the Islamic equivalent of "please God," *deo volente*, and the like. Among Muslims, this is used much more extensively than among Jews or Christians at the present time. To omit it in any statement about the future is regarded as an impiety, even as a provocation. It is sometimes also used with statements about the past, usually to express doubt. An interesting example is provided in a report, preserved in the archives of the Republic of Venice, and sent by its diplomatic envoy in the Ottoman capital, Istanbul. Dated October 1588, the report contains the following passage: "Today the English envoy went to the Pashas and told them that the Spanish armada had been defeated. They said: 'In sha'Allah,' which means"— the astute Venetian diplomat added—"that they didn't believe him."

Their disbelief is understandable, considering the disparity between the mighty Spanish empire and the small island off the coast of Europe. Later, however, the report was confirmed.

Islamic Salvation Front: Commonly known as FIS from its French name, *Front islamique du Salut*. A radical Islamist group in Algeria founded in 1989. In December 1991, it did very well in the first round of elections for the Algerian National Assembly and seemed more than likely to win a clear majority in the second round. In January 1992, amid growing tension, the army canceled the second round and established a military regime. A bitter and bloody struggle followed, and in 1997 Amnesty International assessed the number of victims at 80,000, most of them civilians. It remains a powerful force in Algeria.

Isma'ili: The name of a subsect of the Shi'a (see Chapter 6, "Sunni, Shi'a, and Others").

Jahannum: A place of torment and punishment in the afterlife. In the Koran, it sometimes appears as a synonym of hell or hellfire. The more usual term is *Nar*, literally "fire." In the Islamic perception, hell is made up of a descending sequence of layers. The upper levels are reserved for unrepentant Muslim sinners, the lower for infidels. The torments of hell are described in some detail in the Koran and in later Islamic writings (see *hell*).

Janissary: From the Turkish *yeni cheri*, "new soldiers," the famous Ottoman infantry. These were at first recruited among Christian prisoners of war and then by means of the *devshirme*, a periodic levy of boys from the Christian subject populations of the Empire. This method was abandoned in the 17th century, after which the janissaries became a closed and, increasingly hereditary, corps. As such, it became a strong and to some degree even an independent power within the Ottoman system. An early 19th-century British visitor even called it an Ottoman equivalent of the French Chamber of Deputies—though not, interestingly, of the House of Commons. The corps, seen as an obstacle to reform, was abolished by the Sultan in 1826.

Jizya: The term, in the technical language of Shari'a, for the poll-tax payable by tolerated non-Muslims under Muslim rule. The term already appears in the Koran: "Fight against those who do not believe in God or in the last day, and do not forbid what God and his Prophet have forbidden and do not follow the true faith, until they pay the jizya from the hand, and humbly" (9:29). Its payment continued to be an essential part of the status of *dhimmi* (see pp. 56, 188). The methods of assessment and collection varied from time to time and from place to place. By the 19th century, the idea of a poll-tax on people of another faith was no longer acceptable to enlightened modern opinion. There was, however, a temporary solution. Another aspect of the dhimma was a ban on bearing arms, and the poll-tax could thus be conveniently replaced by a military service exemption tax. At the present time, both the ban and poll-tax have been relinquished (see pp. 56-57).

Ka'ba: Sometimes known as the house of God, *bayt Allah*, a cube-like building situated in the center of the Great Mosque in Mecca. It is the central and most respected sanctuary of Islam. The door of the facade, facing northeast, is about two meters above ground level and can be reached by wooden steps on wheels. The Black Stone is in the eastern corner. Muslims all over the world pray in the direction of the Ka'ba, and every year, pilgrims make it the focal point of their pilgrimage. According to the Koran (2:125–127), the foundations of the Ka'ba were laid by Abraham (Ibrahim) and his son Ishmael (Isma'il) (see photo, p. 19).

Kafir: An Arabic word meaning "unbeliever," from a verb meaning "to disbelieve or deny." The Turkish form is *gavur*. It is the term commonly used in Arabic and other Islamic languages to denote non-Muslims. Islamic law and practice make an important distinction between two categories of unbelievers: The first consists of monotheists to whom at some time in the past God sent prophets who brought books of revelation. In principle, this category consisted of Jews, Christians, and a third group known as the Sabaeans or *Sabi'a* (see pp. 210-211). For many centuries now, it has been limited to Jews and Christians, and the books in question to the Old and New Testaments. These, when they come under the authority of the Muslim state, may be accorded the status of *dhimmi* (see p. 188). The second category are those who have no book—or at least none recognized by Islam as of divine origin—and who worship false or plural gods. These, according to the holy law, may not be accorded tolerance, but must be given the choice of conversion or death. The latter may, however, be commuted to enslavement. Some have suggested that the term *kafir* should apply only to the second and not to the first category, but in general, it has been applied to both (see *takfir*).

Khamsin: An Arabic word meaning 50. The name of a hot windstorm from the south or southeast that blows periodically in the spring.

Khan: A Turko-Mongol princely title, probably a contraction of *khaqan*. In both forms, the title occurs at an early date but is best known through its adoption by the great Mongol conqueror Jengiz and his successors. It was also used by others exercising sovereign authority, among them the Ottoman sultans. Like other titles, it underwent a process of gradual devaluation. Among the Turks and Arabs, it has disappeared; in Iran and Central Asia, it survived rather longer as an equivalent of "mister." It sometimes appears as a family name. Khan is also used to designate a large building for the accommodation of travelers and their wares. In this sense, it is the equivalent of caravanserai (see *caravan*).

Khanum (sometimes written **Hanum** and **Hanim**): A feminine form of the Turko-Mongol Khan. Like its masculine equivalent, it has gradually declined from a princely title to a polite form of address for ladies.

Khatib: The preacher in the mosque who delivers the *Khutba* (see p. 43).

Khawaja: In Egyptian dialect, *Khawaga*. At one time widely used in the Arabic-speaking countries as a polite form of address for foreigners, specifically non-Arab, non-Muslim foreigners. The word is derived from the Persian *Khaja*, a term used as a specially respectful form of address—to a rich merchant, a senior scholar or teacher, a venerable old man, a lord or master, a vizier or other high dignitary of state. It is also used, perhaps ironically, to address a eunuch. The Turkish form *hoca*, pronounced "hodja," is used to address or refer to a Muslim man of religion, or, in a secular context, to a teacher. A famous example is the Hodja Nasreddin Efendi, hero of a rich folklore of humorous anecdotes.

Khutba: The sermon preached in the mosque during the public, communal prayer on Fridays. In early times, this was often a political statement made by or on behalf of the sovereign or administrative head of the area. Later, it became a predominately religious ceremony and was delivered by a preacher known as the *Khatib* (see p. 43).

Kismet: A Turkish word used in the general sense of fate or destiny. It derives from the Arabic Qisma, meaning a share or allocation. From this, it acquired the meaning of portion, and hence, of the preordained fate of each individual. For Muslim views on predestination, see p. 73.

Levant: From an Italian word meaning sunrise; from the late middle ages used particularly of the eastern shores and islands of the Mediterranean.

Levantine: This term is principally used nowadays in a negative sense, to evoke some of the less attractive features attributed to Middle Easterners in business and politics, and especially in the area—always important in the Middle East, and sometimes dominant—where the two intersect.

In earlier times, the term had a different and more precise connotation and was primarily used of a large and important community that played a significant role in East/West relations from the 16th to the 19th century. They lived in the cities, principally the seaports of the Levant and some of the adjoining regions. They were a mixture of families of (mostly south) European origin, long settled in Middle Eastern countries, and of more or less Westernized members of the non-Muslim minorities living under Muslim rule. These were overwhelmingly Christian, members of the Catholic, Greek, and various Eastern churches. Westernized Middle Eastern Jews were sometimes included in this category, but generally speaking it was Christian. Some Levantine families were of European origin; others—many more—had somehow managed to acquire the status of protected subjects of a European state, and thus benefit from the capitulations (see pp. 184-185). Even where they could not claim citizenship of foreign powers, they were often able to obtain some measure of protection, through the status claimed and exercised by certain European governments as protectors of Christian subjects of the Ottoman Empire. From the late 18th century, the Russians, beginning with the "protection" of a small orthodox church in Istanbul, built this up into a protectorate of the Orthodox Christian populations of the whole empire. The French paralleled this with a similar claim to patronage and protection over the Catholic population of the Ottoman Empire. For the contending European powers, this established right of involvement and interference in the internal affairs of the Empire was a useful source of influence and even power. Britain, the other main contender for influence and power in the Middle East, was at a disadvantage, since the Protestant populations of the empire were insignificant. Some attempts were made in course of the 19th century and after to adopt the Jews as a substitute beneficiary of British protection.

At a time when Westerners knew little of the Middle East, and Middle Easterners knew even less of the West, Levantines often played an important role in both politics and commerce. Both the Middle Eastern governments and the foreign embassies and corporations made use of them, albeit with some reserve and even contempt. In Ottoman usage, they were sometimes spoken of as "freshwater Franks," as opposed to the saltwater, that is, "real" Franks from Western Europe. A vivid example of how they were seen by a Westerner may be found in a book published in 1832 by a British naval officer, Adolphus Slade, who spent much of his career in the Levant. "By a Levantine is meant a Frank who has totally abandoned his native country, and fixed himself in Turkey for good. He cannot be mistaken. He is a compound of the Turk, the Greek, and the Frank: disfigured by the mustache of the first, the long hair of the second, the whiskers and dress of the third; not the dress usually worn in Europe, but a mixture of fashions for the preceding half century; no wonder that the Easterners think it unbecoming. He talks many languages—none well: he is servile with Muslims, pert with Christians—your humble servant abroad, a tyrant at home." Half a century later, an American ambassador to Turkey, in a book published in 1887, remarked that "even the vocal organs of the Levantine seem to be polyglot."

Madrasa: See p. 48.

Maghreb (more correctly **maghrib**): An Arabic term literally meaning "the place or time of the sunset." It is used to denote the sunset prayer, and sometimes in the general sense of west or occident. Its most common use in Arabic is to denote the region of Muslim northwest Africa, including Morocco, Algeria, Tunisia, and, sometimes though not usually, Libya.

Mahdi: An Arabic term literally meaning "the rightly guided one," that is to say, "guided by God." According to a Muslim belief that is widely held though not grounded in the Koran, the Mahdi is a Messianic figure who will come at the end of time to establish justice and restore the faith. There have been many claimants to this title and office in the course of Muslim history.

Mahr: Sometimes loosely translated "dowry." In Islamic law, the mahr is a kind of bridal gift given by the bridegroom to his bride, whose property it becomes (see pp. 114-115).

Maliki: A follower of the school of Malik ibn Anas (see p. 30).

Mameluke (correctly **mamluk**): An Arabic word with the literal meaning of "owned," that is to say, a slave. In time it was specialized to denote white slaves as distinct from black slaves who were called 'abd (plural 'abid) (see p. 179). These white slaves were recruited especially for military, and hence also for administrative and political purposes. Mamluk soldiers were usually led by Mamluk officers and commanded by Mamluk generals, some of whom founded Mamluk sultanates. The most famous of these ruled Egypt as an independent state from 1250 to 1517 and continued to dominate the country even after the Ottoman conquest, until their sway was ended by the double blow, first of the French occupation in 1798, and then the rule of Muhammad Ali Pasha in the early 19th century. In European usage, this word, often spelled *mameluke*, was normally used in its original Middle Eastern connotation.

There are, however, exceptions. In early 16th-century Italy, *mammalucco* was used for certain fighting slaves of the Pope and other rulers; while in modern Italy it is sometimes used to mean blockhead or dolt. Much the same meaning is also conveyed in Spanish and Portuguese. Brazilian Portuguese adds a new twist, applying the term to the offspring of a European father and a native American mother. In Danish, *mamelukker* was the common term for the frilly long drawers worn by young girls in the 19th century—the kind known in the United States at that time as pantalettes. This is presumably based on a perceived resemblance between pantalettes and the costume of the Mamluks in the East.

Mihrab: The niche in the wall of the mosque indicating the direction of prayer (see Chapter 4, "The Mosque").

Minaret: A tower, usually attached to a mosque (see photo, p. 42).

Minbar: A pulpit or similar structure in the mosque (see p. 43).

Monsoon: A word borrowed from Arabic via India, where it was picked up and brought to Europe, first by the Portuguese, and then by the Dutch, the French, and other Western nations active in Asia in the 16th and 17th centuries. It comes from the Arabic word *mawsim*, which simply means season and was used to designate the periodic winds and heavy rainfall in the south Asian seas.

Muezzin: See p. 42.

Mufti: An Arabic word literally meaning "one who is competent to issue a fatwa" (see p. 205). The mufti was originally a kind of freelance juris-consult. In Ottoman times, it became the common practice to appoint a mufti to a city, district or province, as chief authority in the area in matters concerned with the holy law of Islam, the Shariʿa. This practice was retained in the post-Ottoman states of the Middle East.

Mukhtar: An Arabic word literally meaning "chosen." In the 19th century, the term was adopted in the Ottoman Empire to designate the head-man of a village or of a city neighborhood. The mukhtar, who was almost invariably a local man, served in many ways as a link between the people and the central government. At some times and places, the mukhtar was chosen locally, by some form of election, or, more precisely, consensus among the local leading families. At other times, more especially with the process of modernization, he was appointed from above. The system continued in many of the successor states after the breakup of the Ottoman Empire.

Mullah or **Mollah**: A Persian word derived from the Arabic *mawla* which, among many other meanings, was used in the sense of lord, master, or patron. In this sense, it has been used politically, such as in Morocco, where many of the sultans prefixed the word *mawlay*, "my master," to their names, and religiously, especially in Iran, for religious teachers and leaders. It is often used in Iran and in some other places to designate professional men of religion in general.

Murtadd: The technical Islamic term for an apostate, that is, one who has renounced Islam.

According to the holy law as traditionally understood, this is a capital offense, and the offender must be put to death, whatever the circumstances. Even if he later repents and reverses his apostasy, he must still be executed. God may forgive him, but no human authority is empowered to do so. This penalty applies even in the case of a new convert to Islam, of however brief duration, who reverts to his previous faith. The death penalty normally included not only the convert but also anyone responsible for converting him. According to the proponents of *taqiya* (see pp. 219-220), the apostate may be forgiven if his apostasy is forced and false. In addition to a formal renunciation of the faith, some actions, such as certain forms of blasphemy, are considered tantamount to apostasy, and incur the same penalties.

Despite the impossibility of even attempting to convert Muslims, Christian missions of various churches were extremely active under some Muslim governments, notably under the Ottoman Empire. Their purpose was to convert Jews to Christianity and, more especially, to convert Christians from one church to another. During the long and bitter struggle between Protestants and Catholics in Europe, both sides became aware that there was a large, untapped reservoir of Christians in the Islamic lands, not committed to either of the contending Western churches. Most of the Middle Eastern Christians belonged to one or other of the Eastern churches—Orthodox, Armenian, Coptic, Syrian, etc. For a while, Catholic missions achieved some success in supporting or creating Uniate Churches, that is, autonomous churches with their own rules and rites but in communion with Rome. The best known of these is the Maronite Church of Lebanon. The Protestant missions also succeeded in winning converts from among the Eastern churches. Under the rule of the Western empires, the missionaries had free reign. Since the ending of Western imperial rule, their activities had been more circumscribed and in some countries, in accordance with the old laws, totally forbidden. In general, by conversion to Islam and emigration, the ancient Christian communities of the Middle East have been dwindling steadily.

Muslim Brothers: In Arabic, *al-Ikhwan al-Muslimun*, a militant, radical, Islamist movement. Founded in 1928 by the Egyptian schoolmaster Hasan al-Banna, it has become the most powerful opposition group in Arab and other Muslim countries. The Muslim Brothers have been particularly active in opposing secular regimes, even anti-Western nationalist regimes, seen by them as undermining the faith. In December 1948, they were accused of responsibility for the assassination of the Egyptian Prime Minister, Mahmud Fahmi al-Nokrashi, as well as some other assassinations. Severe measures were taken against them. In 1966, Sayyid Qutb, one of the intellectual leaders of the movement and a major figure in modern Islamist thought, was executed in Egypt on a charge of plotting the assassination of President Nasser.

An even more dramatic clash occurred in the Syrian city of Hama in 1982. The troubles began with an uprising headed by the local Muslim Brothers. The Syrian government responded swiftly and violently, first attacking the city with tanks, artillery, and bomber aircraft, and following these with bulldozers to complete the work of destruction. A large part of the city was reduced to rubble and the number killed was estimated by Amnesty International at somewhere between 10,000 and 25,000. Curiously and significantly, at the time, this evoked little comment and less protest in the Muslim world or in the wider international community.

Since then, there has been no comparable massacre, but the party's political activities, such as participation in elections, have been subject to obstruction and harassment. More recently, the leaders of the Muslim Brothers have sought to differentiate themselves from more violent and terrorist Islamic groups, preferring rather to portray themselves as "peaceful" and even as "democratic" reformists.

Narghile: See *Hookah*.

Niqab: A kind of veil worn by Sunni women influenced by the Muslim Brotherhood, the Salafiyya, and the Wahhabis. Only the eyes show, but there is a piece of material on top of the head so if the woman wishes to cover her eyes she can pull it down over them.

Nizari: The largest and most active group of the Isma'ili (see pp. 63-64) sect of Islam. They are named after Nizar, the eldest son of the Fatimid Caliph al-Mustansir (died 1094). When Nizar's younger brother succeeded to the Fatimid caliphate in Cairo, they became an opposition group in exile. They were active in the Yemen, then in Iran, Syria, and other places. In India and Pakistan, they are known as Khojas. The most celebrated branch was that of the militant medieval group known in the West as the Assassins (see pp. 181-182). At the present time, Nizari communities are found in Central Asia, the Indian subcontinent, the Middle East, as well as emigre communities in Africa and North America. Their hereditary leader is the Aga Khan (see p. 180 and *Isma'ili*, p. 198).

Organization of the Islamic Conference: Founded in 1969, it is composed of 57 states. Its declared purpose is to strengthen solidarity and cooperation among Islamic states in the political, economic, cultural, scientific, and social fields. Under its charter, it also aims to safeguard the Holy Places, support the struggle of the Palestine people, and work to eliminate racial discrimination and all forms of colonialism. A not insignificant number of states were accepted as members on the basis of Muslim minorities; these include two states in the Western hemisphere—Surinam and Guyana—admitted to membership in 1996 and 1998, respectively. One member, Albania, is in Europe; the remainder are in Asia and Africa. The Turkish Cypriot Authority and Bosnia-Herzegovina were admitted to observer status in 1979 and 1994, respectively. The Palestine Authority was admitted to full membership from the very beginning of the organization in 1969.

Ottoman Empire: The last and most enduring of the great Islamic empires. Founded by a Turkish chieftain named Osman (variant reading, "Othman" hence the European name Ottoman), it began at the turn of the 13th to 14th centuries as one of a number of Turkish principalities in Asia Minor and expanded by conquest until it included the Middle East west of Iran, North Africa as far as the frontier of Morocco, and a rapidly growing part of southeastern and, for a while, central Europe. In May 1453, the Ottoman Sultan Mehmet II, known as the Conqueror, captured the ancient city of Constantinople, which, now commonly known as Istanbul, became and remained the capital of the Empire. Sometime later, the Ottoman Sultans assumed the title "Caliph," implying a claim to Islamic leadership. The Ottomans controlled the Holy Places of Islam from 1517 until World War I.

While Ottoman armies laid siege to the cities of central Europe, corsairs from North Africa waged naval jihad against the seaports and shipping of western Europe. Twice, in 1529 and 1683, Ottoman armies besieged Vienna, the capital of the Holy Roman Empire. On both occasions, they failed. The first failure opened a period of stalemate; the second inaugurated a long and hard-fought Ottoman withdrawal from their European conquests.

The final defeat came at the end of World War I, in which the Ottomans fought on the side of the Central powers. In 1918, their territories were conquered and their capital occupied by the victorious allies, who planned to divide the Ottoman realm among themselves. A Turkish patriotic rising led by Mustafa Kemal, later surnamed Atatürk, preserved the independence of the Turkish heartland and liberated Istanbul. But his aim was to establish a secular republic, not to restore the empire. Under his rule, the Sultanate and then the Caliphate were abolished, and in 1924, the last Ottoman caliph went into exile.

Paradise: From the Greek *paradeisos*, used by Xenophon to describe the parks and gardens of the kings of Persia, derived from the ancient Persian *pairidaeza*, an enclosed area. The term is applied in the Bible to the Garden of Eden, and more broadly, to the abode of the blessed in heaven. The usual Arabic term is *janna*, literally garden.

The delights of paradise (for males) are described in some detail in the Koran (52; 55; 56; 76, etc.) and in still greater and more explicit detail in the early traditions and commentaries. The Koranic paradise has lush and bountiful gardens with rivers of wine, honey, and milk, and water flowing constantly. Trees without thorns bear a multitude of flowers and fruits and their shade is long extended. The blessed will recline on thrones with green cushions, resting on beautiful carpets lined with rich brocade. They will wear garments of silk, have vessels of silver and crystal goblets, and these cups will be full. Never will they suffer from indigestion or drunkenness. They will be attended by *houris*, chaste maidens who restrain their glances, and whom no man or genie has touched before them, and also by youths "like hidden pearls."

Pasha: A Turkish title of disputed etymology, dating from the Middle Ages. In the Ottoman Empire, it was the highest title of honor given to a subject. It was accorded more or less automatically to the governors of provinces, and thus came to be used at times as a synonym of "governor." Like other Turkish titles, it did not precede but followed the name, for example, Ahmed Pasha. Unlike European titles, it was not hereditary and conferred no rank on either wives or children. The title was abolished by the Turkish Republic but was still conferred for a while by the sovereigns of Egypt and Transjordan. In the modern Middle East, it is no longer conferred or used as an official title but may still be encountered—more jocularly than seriously—to designate men or rank, power and/or importance.

Qadi: Sometimes transcribed *Kadi*, a judge in a court of Islamic law (see p. 45).

Qibla: The direction of the Ka'ba in Mecca toward which Muslims must turn during the five daily prayers and the communal prayer on Friday. As Islam spread from Arabia to vast regions in the East and the West, determining the qibla was sometimes an important problem requiring mathematical calculations (see pp. 14, 39).

Qiyama: Literally, "resurrection." The Koran refers in a number of places to *yawm al-qiyāma*, the day of resurrection. This is preceded by the destruction of all the living and followed by the day of final judgment (*yawm al-din*).

Ramadan: The ninth month in the Muslim calendar during which Muslims are required to fast between sunrise and sunset (see pp. 16-17).

Sabaeans, Sabi'a: In mandating tolerance for monotheists who have received a previous divine revelation, the Koran mentions three such groups—the Jews, the Christians, and the Sabaeans. The names Jews and Christians are clear and unequivocal, but the Sabaeans, thrice named in the Koran, are somewhat more enigmatic (Koran 2:62; 5:69; 22:17). The name originally seems to have been applied to a Judeo-Christian sect in Mesopotamia, also known as the Mandaeans. The name was later claimed and used by another religious group, probably pagan, in the town of Harran, in a successful attempt to claim the same measure of tolerance as was accorded to the Jews and Christians. After the great Islamic conquests in Asia and Africa, the name was sometimes used to accord the same measure of tolerance to other, previously unknown religions. It is no longer used.

Sahib: An Arabic word with a wide range of related but different meanings. These include 1) companion or associate; 2) owner or possessor, and 3) master or lord. Combined with other words, it is used in titles as the equivalent of excellency, eminence, highness, etc. Passing from Arabic to Persian and from Persian to the various Muslim languages of India, it came to be the title, (pronounced "saab") by which gentlemen, and more especially but not exclusively European gentlemen, were addressed.

Salafiyya: See pp. 158-159.

Salam, Salaam: See p. 8.

Saracen: A word of disputed etymology, used in late Greek and Latin and subsequently in the languages of Christian Europe to designate first the nomadic peoples of the desert adjoining Syria and Iraq, later the Arabs, and eventually the Muslim peoples of the Mediterranean countries in general. The term is now obsolete.

Saray: A Persian word, also commonly used in Turkish. It reached the West in a number of forms, mostly via French and Italian, in the form *serai, serail,* and *seraglio,* the last of these made famous by Mozart's opera, "The Abduction from the Seraglio." In the Islamic lands, it simply means "palace." In Western but not Islamic usage, it was chiefly used to denote the women's quarters of a Muslim house.

Satan: In Arabic, *Shaytan,* he appears frequently in the Koran, especially in the role of tempter, as for example in the final chapter (114) in which the believer is urged "to seek refuge with God from the evil of the insidious tempter, who whispers in the hearts of men." Thus, when Khomeini described the United States as "the Great Satan," he was not alluding to the more common accusations of imperialism, domination, exploitation, and the like, but rather to the dangerous allure of the sinful Western way of life, seen as a threat to the purity of the Islamic faith and order (see also *Iblis*).

Saudi Arabian Kingdom: Formally constituted by this name by a royal decree in 1932. Its earlier history can be traced back to the mid-18th century when Muhammad Ibn Saud, a tribal chieftain from the region of Riyadh, joined with Muhammad Ibn Abd al-Wahhab, a religious leader and founder of what came to be known as Wahhabism (see pp. 157-158).

The modern history of the House of Saud begins in 1902 when Abd al-Aziz Ibn Saud, commonly known simply as Ibn Saud, recaptured the oasis town of Riyadh, formerly held by members of his family. This was the first major step in the expansion which brought most of the Arabian peninsula under Ibn Saud's rule. In 1925 to 1926, he was able to conquer the Hijaz (see p. 195), ousting the Hashimites who had ruled it for centuries and making the most sacred sites of Islam part of his realm. He was declared King of the Hijaz in 1926 and proclaimed the Saudi Arabian Kingdom in 1932.

The Kingdom now comprises more than 80 percent of the Arabian peninsula with an estimated population of more than 27 million. It derives enormous prestige in the Islamic world from its successful custodianship of the two holiest places of Islam, Mecca and Medina, and its control of the pilgrimage which brings millions of Muslims from all over the world to these cities. Since the 1960s, the monarchy has acquired vast wealth from the exploitation of its immense oil reserves. The Saudi oil company, Aramco, is the world's largest producer of oil. The combination of religious fervor, political influence, and boundless wealth has given the Saudi Kingdom enormous influence all over the Islamic world and beyond.

According to the Saudi basic law proclaimed in 1992, the Koran is the constitution of the country, Shari'a the law of the land. In the Hijaz, except for the seaport of Jedda, no non-Muslim is permitted to set foot. In the rest of the Kingdom, non-Muslims are permitted and are indeed accepted in increasing numbers to provide essential services. But religious worship of any kind other than Islamic is forbidden, even in private homes. So too is the wearing or display of any non-Islamic religious emblems.

Sayyid: A title of honor, roughly equivalent to lord or master. In the past, it was usually though not invariably restricted to the descendants of the Prophet. In modern times, it has come to be used much more widely, and at the present day is no more than the equivalent of "mister" (see also *Sharif*).

Sepoy: From the Persian *sipahi*, a "horseman," hence a cavalryman, sometimes more loosely used of soldiers in general. From Persian, the word moved via Urdu to India and via Turkish to North Africa. In both places it was used by the imperial powers—by the British in India in the form *sepoy*, by the French in Algeria in the form *spahi*—to designate the native troops in their service. The terms *askari* and *lascar* are sometimes used in the same sense. Both of these derive from the Arabic *askar* or, with the definite article, *al-askar*, an Arabic word meaning "army," itself probably derived from the Latin word for army—*exercitus*. Since the passing of the European empires, these terms have become in effect obsolete.

The Indian mutiny of 1857 to 1859, among Indian troops in the British army, is known as the "Sepoy Mutiny" because it was started by sepoys. According to a story current at the time, they were provoked to revolt by a report, probably untrue, that their cartridges were greased with pig fat.

Shafi'i: The name of the Sunni school of theology and law founded by Abu Abdallah Muhammad al-Shafi'i (767–820 CE) (see p. 31 and Chapter 5, "Diversity and Tolerance").

Shah: The old Persian word for king, used by the monarchs of ancient Iran and revived in Islamic times. It disappeared with the dethronement of the last Shah of Iran and the abolition of the monarchy in that country in 1979. Shahanshah, "king of kings," conveys the meaning of supreme monarch or emperor. This way of indicating hierarchic supremacy dates back to ancient Iran and was retained after the advent of Islam. The chief *kadi* was the kadi of kadis; the chief *amir* was the amir of amirs. In Turkish, the governor-general of a group of provinces was called the Beylerbey, that is, the *bey* of beys. The title adopted by the bishops of Rome, *Servus Servorum Dei*, the Servant of the Servants of God, may be a distant echo of this practice.

Shahid: Usually translated martyr, from an Arabic verb meaning to bear witness or to testify. At the present time, it is used commonly to denote the new phenomenon of the suicide bomber (see p. 153). *Shahid* is the linguistic equivalent of the Greek word *martys*, "witness," from which our word martyr is derived. The Muslim conception of martyrdom is, however, somewhat different from that of either the Jews or the Christians. In the words of the *Oxford English Dictionary*, a martyr is "one who voluntarily undergoes the penalty of death for refusing to renounce the Christian faith…one who undergoes death (or great suffering) on behalf of any belief or cause, or through devotion to some object." In the Muslim perception, a shahid is one who gives his life fighting for the faith—in other words, in a holy war. The shahid enjoys special rewards in heaven (see *Paradise*).

A word from the same root, *shahada*, in the sense of testifying to the true faith, is one of the five pillars of Islam (see Chapter 2, "The Pillars of the Faith").

Shari'a: An Arabic word with the primary meaning of "a path leading to a watering place." It was used figuratively and now almost exclusively to denote the holy law of Islam, which in principle regulates all aspects of communal and personal life—religious and ritual, civil and criminal, public and private (see Chapter 3, "Scripture, Tradition, and Law").

Sharif: A term with the general meaning "noble or high born," applied particularly to descendants and kinsmen of the Prophet. In medieval, Ottoman, and early modern times, it came to be the regnal title of the Amirs of Mecca until they were ousted and their realm taken over by

Ibn Saud in 1925–1926. The title sharif has also been used by the royal house of Morocco.

Sheikh or **Shaykh**: An Arabic word meaning "old man." This term is frequently mispronounced. To achieve an approximately correct pronunciation, one should pronounce the first part rather like the English word "shake," and the final consonant like the "ch" in the Scottish Loch. At a time and in a place when older men were presumed to have greater wisdom and were, therefore, entrusted with greater power, the word also acquired the connotations of leadership, dignity, and authority. Among the Bedouin Arabs, a sheikh has been since remote antiquity, and still is today, the head of the tribe. In some of the principalities of modern Arabia, it has been used as a hereditary title of rulers. Such territories are sometimes called sheikhdoms.

After the advent of Islam, sheikh also came to be used as the title of a religious dignitary, especially a graduate of a theological seminary. It was also applied to the heads of religious orders and fraternities and sometimes also of craft guilds, often associated of such fraternities. The title "Sheikh al-Islam"—literally "the old man of Islam"—was in medieval times conferred by consensus on eminent theologians. Under the Ottomans, it was the official title of the Chief Mufti of Istanbul, the head of the entire religious establishment of the Empire. A similar but not identical semantic development in the usage of words connoting old age may also be observed in English. From the Anglo-Saxon "old," we get elders and aldermen; from the Latin *senex*, an old man, came senior, senator—and senile.

Shi'a: An Arabic word primarily meaning party or faction. It was first applied to a legitimist group supporting the claims of Ali, the son-in-law and cousin of the Prophet, to succeed him as head of the Muslim community. During the struggles of early Islamic history, the Shi'a developed into a religious movement, differing on a number of points from Sunni Islam. At the present time, the Shi'a are the second-largest group among Muslims, after the Sunnis. They form the majority of the population in Iran and Iraq, as well as significant groups in Syria and Lebanon, and in central and south Asia (see *Imam* and Chapter 6, "Sunni, Shi'a, and Others").

Shi'i or **Shi'ite**: A follower of the Shi'a (see Chapter 6).

Slavery: In the Koran, as in both the Old and New Testaments, slavery is taken as a fact of life, and attempts are made, in various ways, to lighten the lot of the slave or slavewoman and protect them against cruelty or misuse. Liberating slaves is meritorious but is not a requirement, though it may in certain cases be imposed as a penalty for some offense. In premodern times, in the Islamic world as elsewhere, slaves played an important part in the society and the economy. In addition—and this is more distinctive—they also played a major role in the military and, hence, the state. Before long, we find not only slave-soldiers, but also slave-generals and, in due course, slave-dynasties.

According to Islamic law, a free person residing in the Islamic lands, whether a Muslim or a *dhimmi* (see p. 188), could not be enslaved. The slave population was, therefore, recruited in two ways. One was by birth. The children of slave parents were born slaves and remained so unless or until they were set free by their owners. A special case was that of the *umm walad*, a slave concubine who bore a child to her free Muslim owner.

The second source of recruitment to the slave population was by importation from outside the Islamic lands. This again could happen in two ways, by purchase or by capture. In premodern times, the slave trade was a vast and complex commercial enterprise, by which great numbers of slaves were brought from Europe, Asia, and Africa into the Islamic lands. The other method of recruitment from abroad was by capture. This was in principle limited to the *jihad*, the holy war against the infidels, in which the holy warrior was permitted to keep and use his captives and their families as slaves.

The legal abolition of slavery began in the 19ᵗʰ century, at first in the territories ruled by the European empires, then in the independent states. It was in principle completed in the year 1962, when slavery was legally abolished in Saudi Arabia and Yemen. There are indications that it has not entirely disappeared, and in some post-imperial societies has even reappeared.

ISLAMIC HUMOR

A certain man became a Shiʿite and went around saying that whoever was not a Shiʿite was a bastard. His son said to him: "But I am not a Shiʿite."

To this the man replied: "Yes indeed. I bedded your mother before I bought her."

Sublime Porte: An English literal mistranslation of the French translation of an Ottoman term (Bab-i ʿAli); literally, "the high or lofty door." It was used to symbolize the office of the Grand Vizier, the central authority of the Ottoman government. One speaks of "The White House" or "Downing Street" in the same way.

It is told that a Grand Vizier in the mid-19ᵗʰ century invited the foreign Ambassadors and their wives to a reception in the palace. As was usual, the wives of the Ambassadors were offered a tour of the harem. One of the Ambassadors, apparently unaware of Muslim customs, asked if he could join the tour. The Grand Vizier replied (in French), "You are accredited to the 'Porte' (door), but not beyond the 'porte.'"

Sufi: Commonly used to to denote Muslim Mystics (see pp. 67-69).

Suicide: At the present time suicide, and more specifically the suicide terrorist, has come to be regarded as something characteristically and distinctively Islamic. In the past, for most of the recorded history of Islam and of Islamic states and societies, the exact opposite was true. In some civilizations, such as ancient Rome and traditional Japan, suicide is not only an acceptable choice; it is even, in certain situations, an obligation of honor. In most Christian countries, suicide is classified as both a sin and a crime, but despite this, it was generally regarded as an acceptable choice in certain situations, and suicides are not infrequent in the history of Christendom.

In the Islamic world, for most of Islamic history, suicide is so rare as to be almost unknown. The classical Islamic view, as laid down and elaborated in both juristic and theological literature, is that suicide is a major sin, earning eternal damnation.

References to suicide in the Koran are few and indirect, and they have been variously interpreted. The traditions of the Prophet however, and the whole theological and juristical tradition based on them, are unequivocal. Suicide is a major sin and however virtuous a life the one who commits it may have led, he forfeits any claim to paradise and condemns himself to hell, where, according to tradition, his punishment will consist of the eternal repetition of the act of suicide.

At a certain stage, the question was posed and debated: "Is it permissible in a jihad for a man to throw himself against a vastly superior enemy, knowing that this will lead to certain death?" The general view was that this is permissible, because he does not die by his own hand. A case in point is the Assassins (see pp. 152-153, 181-182) who made no attempt to escape after killing their victim, but never died by their own hands.

In the modern period, new doctrines on the one hand, and new weaponry on the other, posed a new question—the lawfulness or otherwise of the suicide bomber. The extremist view, adopted and expounded in the Salafi and Wahhabi (see pp. 157-158) literature is that this is not only permissible, it is meritorious provided that he takes a number of enemy infidels with him. The more traditional view would be that anyone who dies by his own hand, in whatever circumstances, is guilty of the sin of suicide, and thereby earns eternal damnation. For the suicide bombers of today, much rests on a point of interpretation.

Sultan: Originally an Arabic noun meaning rule or power, then personalized to denote the individual who exercises power. It was already used informally in this sense in the 10th century and more formally in the 11th, when it acquired the special meaning of the independent ruler of a definite territory. From then onward, it came to denote the supreme military authority as contrasted with the supreme religious authority embodied in the caliphate. After the destruction of the Abbasid caliphate in Baghdad by the conquering Moguls in 1258 CE, it became the normal title of independent sovereignty used by Muslim rulers.

A few sultans still remain, but in most Muslim countries, the title is no longer in fashion. In some, the sultans were overthrown and replaced by a variety of rulers who styled themselves "president of the republic." In others, while the monarchy was retained, the title sultan was replaced by the more Western, and therefore more prestigious, title of king.

Sunni: One who follows the Sunna, the precept and practice of the Prophet and of the early leaders of Islam, as recorded by tradition (see pp. 29-32). They now form the majority in most Muslim communities and control most Muslim states with the notable exception of Iran. The Christian, originally platonic, term orthodox, "correct belief," is sometimes used to designate the Sunni version of Islam. This is a misleading analogy. "Mainstream" would be a better description. Sunni Islam, like Rabbinic Judaism, is more concerned with correct practice than with correct belief (see Chapter 6, "Sunni, Shi'a, and Others").

Takfir: The act of denouncing one who claims to be a Muslim as a *kafir* (see pp. 199-200), and thus, in effect, to accuse him of the capital crime of apostasy. In earlier times, takfir was comparatively rare and was only pronounced by a properly constituted religious authority. More recently, the term is used by radical and violent Islamic sects to condemn and silence their more moderate critics and opponents (see *Murtadd*).

Taqiyya: Usually translated dissimulation, the disguising of one's true feelings or beliefs. This is based on a verse in the Koran (16:106) that threatens a mighty punishment for those who, after professing faith in

God, revert to unbelief. The verse does, however, make an exception—for those who do so "under compulsion, their heart remaining firm in the faith." An early commentator explains: "If anyone is compelled and professes unbelief with his tongue, while his heart contradicts him, in order to escape his enemies, no blame falls on him, because God takes His servants as their hearts believe." The doctrine of Taqiyya, while not formally rejected by the Sunnis, was of much more importance in Shi'a doctrine and practice, understandably, since at most times and in most places the Shi'a were the minority, and subject to the domination of the Sunni majority or in any case of Sunni rulers. Originally referring only to matters of religious belief and practice, the notion of *taqiyya* has been given a much wider extension today.

A classical example cited by the jurists is a certain Ammar ibn Yasir (Ammar the son of Yasir), an early convert to Islam in Mecca who was severely tortured because of his beliefs and is said to have made some partial recantation. Later he escaped to Ethiopia, and from there rejoined the Prophet in Medina, where he played an active role in the early Islamic state. The name Abu Ammar ("Father of Ammar") sometimes used by the late Yasir Arafat, was an evocation of this early Islamic hero.

Tobacco: A product of the Western hemisphere, tobacco was unknown in the Islamic world until it was introduced by English merchants at the beginning of the 17th century. The habit spread very rapidly.

Some of the more conservative Ulema objected to both tobacco and coffee and issued decrees against them, with little or no effect. In 1633, the austere and severe Sultan Murad IV prohibited both coffee and tobacco and executed a number of smokers and coffee drinkers. But the struggle against tobacco was hopeless, and smoking was finally declared lawful, and in accordance with the laws of Islam, in a fatwa by the chief mufti, himself a heavy smoker who had been dismissed and exiled for smoking some years earlier. Thereafter, smoking in various forms (see *hookah*) became general in the Islamic world, and tobacco was grown in a number of places, notably in Turkey. Indeed, Turkish tobacco became a major export item.

The war against smoking was resumed at a later date by the austere and fanatical Wahhabis, who considered it a form of intoxication and, therefore, a breach of basic Islamic principles.

INTRODUCTION OF TOBACCO

From an early 17th century Turkish historian on the introduction of tobacco to Turkey:

"Many even of the great Ulema and the mighty fell into this addiction. From the ceaseless smoking of the riffraff, the coffee houses were filled with blue smoke, to such a point that those who were in them could not see one another. In the markets and the bazaars, their pipes never left their hands. Puffing in each other's faces and eyes, they made the streets and markets stink. In its honor, they even composed and declaimed silly verses. Sometimes I had arguments with friends about it. I said: 'Its terrible smell taints a man's beard and turban, the clothes on his back and the room wherever it is used; sometimes it even sets fire to carpets, felts, and bedding, and dirties them from end to end with cinders and ash. After sleep, its evil smell rises to the brain...its constant use prevents men from working and earning money...in view of this and other similar harmful and abominable effects, what pleasure or profit can there be in this?' To this, the only answer they could give was: 'It is a pleasure and moreover a pleasure of aesthetic taste.' This is no answer; it is pure pretense. By the beginning of the year 1045 (1635–1636 CE), its spread and fame were more than can be written or expressed."

—Ibrahim Peçevi

Ulema: Correctly *ulama*, the Arabic plural of *alim*, "scholar" and, more particularly, "a specialist in religious subjects, principally theology and law." The term ulema has found its way into Western languages, where it is used to designate the Muslim establishment of professional men of religion including muftis, qadis, and others.

Umma: An Arabic word usually denoting a religious community. In modern usage, it is also used to translate the term "nation," as, for example, in the Arabic name of the United Nations. When one speaks of "the Umma" without specific qualification or designation, it is usually understood to mean the global Muslim community as a whole.

Veil: See Chapter 11, "Women in Islam" and also *Abaya, Burqa, Chador, Niqab*.

Vizier: From the Arabic *wazir*, probably of Persian origin, denoting a high officer of the state under various Muslim regimes. In its earliest occurrences, it describes the chief executive and head of chancery of the administration under the caliphs. Under later Muslim dynasties, the office, and with it the title, underwent several changes. In the Ottoman state, the vezirate initially included high military command. There were several viziers, the first or chief vizier being the *Vezir-A'zam* or *Sadr A'zam*, known in Europe as the "Grand Vizier." He was the supreme head of the Ottoman administration for civil and military matters alike and was responsible for all aspects of government under the supreme authority of the sultan. The office of the Grand Vizier came to be known as the Bab-i Ali, commonly translated "Sublime Porte." During the 19th century, the Grand Vizier gradually dwindled into a Prime Minister, and his office ended with the Ottoman Empire (see Sublime Porte and Ottoman Empire).

Wadi: Defined by the dictionary as "a ravine or gully that occasionally turns into a water course." This derives from the Arabic *wadi*, with the broader meaning of a river-valley in which, depending on the weather, there may or may not be a river. The term is used equally of such mighty rivers as the Nile and the Euphrates and of the normally dry water courses of the Arabian peninsula. On maps of North Africa, the term appears in the form *oued*—a French transcription of the North African dialectal pronunciation of wadi.

Wahhabi: See pp. 69, 157-158.

Waqf (plural **Awqaf**): Usually translated "pious endowment or foundation," a technical term of Islamic law for a kind of trust or endowment, whereby a person sets aside part of his or her property and declares it to be an inalienable trust, at the same time designating the beneficiaries of income accruing from it. Though it is not mentioned in Koran, the waqf is well attested in the traditions of the Prophet and occupies a central position in Shari'a law. So important is the waqf in the economic and social life of Muslim countries, that most modern Muslim states have a separate office or even ministry devoted to the supervision of waqfs, sometimes linked more generally with religious affairs. The beneficiaries of waqfs may be persons, usually relatives and descendants, or they may be a madrasa, mosque, soup-kitchen, water-fountain, or other public utility or charitable institution. The administrators of waqf trusts were normally chosen from among the professional men of religion, and these could at times be a significant instrument of power or influence. The archives contain registers of waqfs, naming the founders, the beneficiaries, and the administrators, and enumerating the assets.

Zaidi: A branch of the Shi'a, usually designated as "moderate," that is, the closest to the Sunnis in doctrine and law. Zaidism has for long been the dominant form of Islam in Yemen.

Index

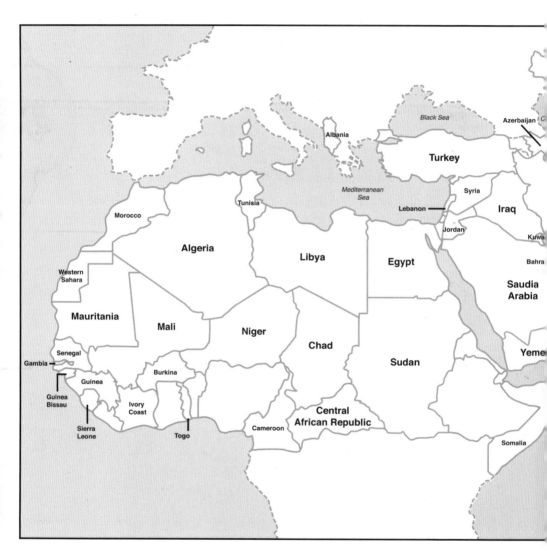

Countries with Majority Muslim Populations